THE
STUDY of SYNTAX

The Generative-Transformational Approach to the Structure of American English

TRANSATLANTIC SERIES in LINGUISTICS
Under the general editorship of
Samuel R. Levin   Hunter College

ANALYTIC SYNTAX
OTTO JESPERSEN

INTRODUCTION TO TAGMEMIC ANALYSIS
WALTER COOK, S.J.
Georgetown University

THE
STUDY of SYNTAX.

The Generative-Transformational Approach to the Structure of American English

D. TERENCE LANGENDOEN
Ohio State University

HOLT, RINEHART AND WINSTON, INC.
New York   Chicago   San Francisco   Atlanta
Dallas   Montreal   Toronto   London   Sydney

To Mamie and Suzie

Acknowledgments

This work was supported, in part, by the Ohio State University Development Fund through its Faculty Fellowship Program.

I would especially like to express my appreciation to the Department of Linguistics of the University of California at San Diego for inviting me to participate in the La Jolla Conference on English Syntax, held February 24–28, 1967, at which many ideas were discussed that, in one form or another, have found their way into this book. I am also indebted to my colleagues Professors Charles J. Fillmore and David L. Stampe for many stimulating discussions on English syntax, and to Professors Gaberell Drachman and Richard Garner for their criticisms of an earlier draft of part of this work. Finally, I would like to express my gratitude to Miss Marlene Deetz for her work in typing the manuscript, and to my wife Sally for her help in preparing the figures and more importantly for her support and encouragement throughout the writing of this work.

Contents

THE
STUDY of SYNTAX

The Generative-Transformational
Approach to the Structure
of American English

1 INTRODUCTION

We may begin our inquiry into the study of SYNTAX[1] by asking what distinguishes a person whom we call fluent in a language, for example English, from one who is not. Fluency clearly involves being able, without noticeable difficulty, to produce (orally or in writing) and to comprehend (by listening or by reading) what are called the SENTENCES of that language. Fluency also involves being able to do these things for sentences that the individual has never before encountered, for we want to distinguish the truly fluent person from one who, like a parrot, has memorized a number of sentences of that language and is able to produce and comprehend just those sentences and no others. In other words, being fluent in a language means being creative in that language, creative not in the sense of artistic creativity but in the sense that one is able to construct or grasp the significance of objects that are totally new. Indeed, being fluent in a language is one of the bases upon which the construction of artistically creative objects of language, such as poems and novels, is founded.[2]

A LANGUAGE may be defined as the collection of sentences that a fluent person would be able to produce or comprehend had he the time, energy, and motivation. From this we conclude that a language is never totally manifested by any individual; in fact, the temporal, physical, and psychological limitations on him are such that in his lifetime he will have actually produced

---

[1] Technical terms in linguistics and other terms that are used in special senses are introduced in small capitals. These terms, along with rudimentary definitions, will be found in the glossary at the end of the book.

[2] For further discussion of this point, see Chomsky (1966, pp. 17–18).

1

and comprehended only an infinitesimal part of his entire language. Moreover, not everything he will have produced in speech and writing or comprehended by listening and reading can be considered sentences of his language. For example, a person may begin speaking, but for some reason break off abruptly before he has finished a sentence. Similarly, many times when one writes, for example a memorandum or a grocery list, one does not write full sentences at all, but rather fragments of sentences and often just words.

At this point it should also be observed that what we are accustomed to think of as "languages," for example English, French, or Japanese, are not languages in the sense defined above. What we call English may be considered to be a family of languages having as many members as there are fluent speakers of what is agreed upon as English. The technical term for the language of a single fluent speaker is IDIOLECT; thus there are as many idiolects of English as there are speakers of English. Now, the differences between the idiolects of any two people from the same geographical area and of the same social standing are bound to be negligible in comparison to their similarities. Such persons will, on the whole, have no difficulties in understanding one another, for they speak the same DIALECT. However, two speakers of English from different geographical areas or of different social standing may readily discover that their languages are different and that although communication is generally possible, some difficulties in understanding what the other one is saying will arise rather frequently. In this case, we say that the two persons are speakers of different dialects. In general, a language such as English is divided along geographical and social lines into a large number of dialects.

To complicate the picture further, there are several dialects which have been singled out as constituting the STANDARD LANGUAGE. Certain of these dialects, which constitute what may be called spoken standard American English, are the only ones acceptable for use in national news broadcasting and for speaking in "polite" (or powerful) society in the United States. The standard language for writing in the United States exists in a number of varieties, two of which can be easily distinguished: formal and informal written standard American English.[3] Spoken standard American English is learned in childhood by the majority of American children, but written standard American English almost always has to be learned in school. Thus written standard American English, and to a lesser extent spoken standard American English, are artificial; many of the criteria which are the

---

[3] For a straightforward discussion of the varieties of written standard American English, see the Introduction to Watt (1967).

basis for determining whether or not particular sentences belong in them are upheld by decree from generation to generation by those who have attained the requisite social standing, and they have been committed to memory by most persons who have gone through school. Conformity to these criteria in both speech and writing is generally the mark of the individual who seeks social power or prestige. The person who has that power or prestige can sometimes afford to revert to his regional nonstandard dialect, at least in speaking.

Returning now to our considerations about the manifestation of language in speech and writing (from this point, the language under consideration will be spoken standard American English, to which we shall refer simply as English), we note that collecting specimens of what people actually say or write, while indeed useful for many purposes, will not lead us to form a very clear picture of what the sentences of English are, since first of all, not all these specimens will be sentences of English, and secondly, the number of sentences actually collected will not even begin to exhaust the totality of English sentences. Furthermore, this collection will tell us very little about the internal structures of English sentences.

In order to obtain information about English which will be useful for determining what are English sentences, and what are their internal structural properties, we require techniques of ELICITATION. Such techniques involve finding out the judgments that speakers of English make about LINGUISTIC OBJECTS[4] that are presented to them. The most common form which elicitation takes is INTROSPECTION. Assuming that the linguist himself is a fluent speaker of English, he may inquire of himself as to what judgments he makes concerning a particular linguistic object. Quite naturally, he runs the risk of misrepresenting these judgments, particularly if the evidence he uncovers does not exactly fit with the rest of the material he has previously collected or examined. But every scientific methodology, even the most "objective," is subject to the same kind of misuse, so that introspection should not be ruled out as a viable technique for someone who rigorously maintains his honesty in his work.

Typical of the judgments that one can elicit are those concerning whether or not a particular linguistic object is or is not an English sentence; that is, whether or not it is GRAMMATICAL in English.[5] Other judgments that one can elicit concern the internal structure of objects regarded as sentences, whether two

---

[4] By a linguistic object, we mean simply any string of words. It may be, but of course need not be, an English sentence.

[5] We shall use in this book the expression E-GRAMMATICAL to designate a sentence of standard American English. A linguistic object which is not a sentence of English will be called E-UNGRAMMATICAL.

or more sentences mean the same thing or not, or whether a particular sentence is subject to a variety of meaningful interpretations or not. Such judgments may be called LINGUISTIC INTUITIONS, and they constitute the raw linguistic data which the student of English syntax must use in his research. Accordingly, Chapter 2 is devoted to a brief investigation of the nature of linguistic data. One important point is that the judgments which constitute those data are more deeply founded than the well-known and explicit grammatical criteria of spoken standard American English found in handbooks of grammar. While it is correct to say that a person "knows" the bases of these judgments, since they can be elicited from him by questioning, he knows them only subconsciously, and if they are pointed out to him, he may evince considerable surprise.

In order to provide a conceptual framework in which to interpret linguistic data, the student of syntax requires a theory of grammar. Among other things, the theory should provide an explicit means of representing those linguistic objects which are found to be sentences of English; that representation, moreover, should include in it all the structural properties of those sentences. The theory should be serviceable as a model of how the language is represented in the mind of an individual, although it will not directly characterize how it is that people actually speak, comprehend, write, and read. Most importantly, the theory should indicate the many and profound ways in which all the languages of the world are similar, and how the languages of humans are different from the forms of communication among nonhumans. Chapter 3 provides the rudiments of such a theory, and an initial attempt is made there to represent some sentences of English using it.

A language serves as a means of communication. Therefore it is more than a system of arbitrarily connected symbols; each of its sentences conveys meaning. One of the tasks of the study of syntax is to determine precisely how it is that sentences convey meaning. This leads us to the study of the meaningfulness of words, and of their combination into sentences. Chapter 4 concerns itself with the nature of meaning. The same meaning, however, can be conveyed by a number of different sentences, while two sentences which look very much alike may be associated with two very different meanings. How this can come about is discussed in Chapter 5.

The last three chapters are concerned with inadequacies in the presentation of Chapters 3–5, particularly in the theory underlying these chapters. In Chapter 6, some modifications in that theory are introduced, and then an attempt is made to classify the sentences of English into a variety of types. Chapter 7 is concerned with some aspects of the relationship between the grammatical structure of sentences and their expression in speech and writing. Finally, Chapter 8 inquires into some of the reasons why the structure of language is as it is, and concludes by providing an indication of the directions in which current research in English syntax is headed.[6]

---

[6] Quite recently a number of excellent introductions to general linguistics written from similar theoretical perspectives as this book have appeared. These include Bolinger (1968), Langacker (1968), and Lyons (1968).

2 THE NATURE OF LINGUISTIC DATA

In Chapter 1, it was maintained that it is not true that whatever an English speaker says or writer writes is a sentence of English. Speech and writing are simply manifestations of a language; a person may have every intention of uttering a fully grammatical sentence in English, but because of the intervention of linguistically irrelevant factors, such as presence of food in the mouth, temporary memory failure, or untimely death, he may not succeed in doing so. On the other hand, we held that fluent speakers of English are, in general, capable, under the proper conditions, of determining for themselves whether particular linguistic objects are or are not fully grammatical sentences in English. The reason they are capable of doing so is that they possess well-developed linguistic intuitions, which constitute the basis of their ability to speak and to comprehend English fluently.

The simplest conditions under which one can elicit judgments of grammaticality for particular linguistic objects is to ask a fluent speaker of English, "Can you say x?" where x is the object under consideration. This technique, however, is unlikely to be successful — there are some agreeable souls who will almost always say "Yes," but who, if pressed further, will admit, for certain objects, that although they could say them, they never would. The failure of this simple technique in many cases to elicit true judgments of grammaticality does not mean, however, that the grammarian should give up in his effort to find out how people think of particular linguistic objects. It means simply that he needs to develop more refined techniques. One possible refinement would be to pose the question thus: "Is there anything odd about x?" or "Is there anything odd about x which you do not find odd about y?" In this way two objects are compared, the second of which has been previously established as not being odd. As an illustration of this technique, I have managed to get a number of speakers of English to agree that the object:[1]

2.1   It's late yet.

is odd in comparison with:

2.2   It's early yet.

whereas these same speakers had previously stated that they "could say" example 2.1. The term "odd" rather than "ungrammatical" was used simply because I did not want to color my subjects' judgments with recollections of their own grade-school conceptions of the notion grammaticality.

However, posing the matter in terms of oddity rather than grammaticality raises other problems. An object may be judged odd simply because it reports a very unlikely state or event in the world of experience, for example:

2.3   I just swallowed my nose.

Yet we would surely want to call example 2.3 E-grammatical. Similarly, an object such as 2.4, which is simply false, may be judged odd by some, but it is certainly not to be considered E-ungrammatical:

2.4   Paris is the capital of Sweden.

But what about objects which are internally contradictory, for example:

2.5   John's sister is the husband of a famous New York attorney.

The oddity of example 2.5 has nothing to do with its truth value; it is odd because it affirms that a particular individual is both male and female — male because someone's husband, female because someone else's sister — which is a contradiction. But is example 2.5 thereby ungrammatical? The answer to that question depends in part at least upon whether one feels that such INTERNAL CONTRADICTION is a matter of the grammar of a language. One consideration that should be borne in mind is that the fact that a linguistic object expresses a contradiction may not be

---

[1] Sentences and other material used as examples to illustrate particular points will be numbered consecutively in each chapter. Sentence 2.1 is thus the first example sentence of Chapter 2. Examples occurring in footnotes will be numbered by small Roman numerals separately within each footnote.

immediately apparent from a casual examination of that object, for example:

2.6 I am eleven years older than my father's brother's son's only cousin.

Internal contradiction can also be seen in the following examples:

2.7 Harry drank a piece of paper.
2.8 The captain stubbed his stomach on a doorknob.
2.9 Misery loves company.

In example 2.7, the verb *drink* occurs, which requires that the expression following it designate a liquid; since a piece of paper is not a liquid, there is a contradiction. The verb *stub* in example 2.8 requires that the following expression designate a toe; since the captain's stomach is not a toe, there is a contradiction. Finally, in 2.9, the verb *love* requires that the expression preceding it be animate, but since misery is not animate, once again there is a contradiction. The standard interpretation of example 2.9, that those who are in misery love to have other miserable persons around them, indicates how people may resolve the internal contradiction inherent in many such linguistic objects. In this example, the abstract noun *misery* has been personified, thus resolving the contradiction. In other cases, the contradiction is resolved by reinterpretation of a verb. Consider for example:

2.10 Joe must be married to that car.

in which the standard reinterpretation is of the verb *marry*, and certainly not of *that car*.[2]

Let us say that we do not consider any of the examples 2.5–2.10 to be *E*-ungrammatical, but that we do take as one of the tasks of syntactic inquiry the determination of the notion of internal contradiction.[3] Ungrammaticality arises not when there is merely internal contradiction within a linguistic object, but when it is felt that the object possesses some gross deformity in comparison with sentences in the language. Consider the fol-

---

[2] I am indebted to Paul Postal for this example.

[3] The explication of the oddity of sentences 2.5–2.10 is properly in the domain of SEMANTICS, or SEMASIOLOGY, the study of the meaning of sentences, which some linguists consider to lie outside the domain of syntax proper. I do not hold to this view; as we shall see, the syntactic analysis of sentences cannot be done without reference to their meanings. Since meaning enters into the problem at all points, it seems appropriate to include among the tasks of syntactic study the explication of the traditional problems of semantics: synonymy, antonymy, paraphrase, contradiction, and so forth. We do not, however, include among the goals of syntactic study the explication of when a particular sentence is appropriate or inappropriate to the external world context in which it is used; for example the oddity of *I see a rabbit* when no rabbit is in view.

lowing examples, which are not to be considered E-grammatical.[4]

2.11 *I forced to go along with me.
2.12 *An untimely arrest took place the riot.

Example 2.11 is judged E-ungrammatical because it is felt that there is a constituent missing from it; compare 2.11 with the E-grammatical example 2.13:

2.13 I forced the child to go along with me.

On the other hand, example 2.12 is ungrammatical because it is felt to have a constituent which it ought not have; compare it with the E-grammatical example 2.14:[5]

2.14 An untimely arrest took place.

The deformity may involve, instead of the presence of unwanted constituents or the absence of required ones, an incorrect order of constituents, as illustrated in the following example:

2.15 *We can only award this prize to very beautiful someone.

Compare with 2.15 the E-grammatical example 2.16:

2.16 We can only award this prize to someone very beautiful.

Or it may involve the presence of an improper form of a part of speech (most such cases involve violations of the explicit standards of English):

2.17 *I hope that everyone has read those book.

In all these examples of E-ungrammatical linguistic objects, it is possible for us to pinpoint the source of the ungrammaticality and to interpret, in some cases at least, these things in terms of E-grammatical objects. However, ungrammatical objects may deviate so grossly from E-grammatical objects that interpretation of them is extremely difficult, if not impossible:

2.18 *Furiously sleep ideas green colorless.

It is also possible to elicit from fluent speakers of English judgments not only about the E-grammaticality of linguistic

---

[4] An asterisk placed in front of an example indicates that it is considered to be E-ungrammatical.

[5] It cannot be emphasized too strongly that the fact that a linguistic object is not E-grammatical does not mean that it is not used (or should not be used) or cannot be understood by fluent speakers of English. Thus, example 2.12 could be used to convey the meaning of a grammatical but very staid sentence such as:

(i) An untimely arrest started the riot.

objects, but also about the internal structures of those objects judged to be grammatical sentences. The simplest judgments that one can elicit concern classification of the words of sentences into "parts of speech," such as NOUN (N),[6] VERB (V), CONJUNCTION (C), and the like, and of the groupings of these elements into PHRASES and CLAUSES. Fluent speakers can also usually be made aware of the patterning of entities within words, for example that a noun such as *boys* consists of two parts — *boy*, which is also identifiable as a noun, and a SUFFIX spelled *s* which indicates plurality. To take a not wholly uninteresting example:[7]

2.19 A few congressmen seem to realize that the administration's present foreign policy is leading the country toward an ultimate direct confrontation with China.

No fluent speakers of English are likely to have difficulty in picking out the nouns (*congressmen, administration's, policy, country, confrontation, China*); similarly the verbs (*seem, realize, is, leading*), although many will rightly point out the auxiliary status of *is* in sentence 2.19. How fluent speakers choose to categorize the other words which appear in 2.19 will no doubt depend at least in part on what grammatical training they have received; there will certainly be disagreement over the status of the word *that* — is it a conjunction, an adverb, or something which is neither of these? We leave these problems aside, to take a look at the intuitions English speakers have of the organization of the sentence into phrases and clauses. The sentence *(S)* as a whole may be broken down into two major phrases: a NOUN PHRASE (NP), *a few congressmen* and a VERB PHRASE (VP), *seem to realize . . . with China*.[8] These phrases function as the SUBJECT and PREDICATE, respectively, of the sentence as a whole. The constituents of the subject NP are the ARTICLE (Art) *a*, the ADJECTIVE (Adj) *few*, and the noun *congressmen*, so nothing further need be said about its internal structure. The predicate VP, on the other hand, can be further analyzed as being made up of a verb *seem* and another VP *to realize . . . with China;* this VP in turn is analyzable as a verb *to realize* and a clause *that . . . with China.* If we reflect

---

[6] Abbreviations for the various grammatical categories that will be used in this book are introduced with the first mention of each category. Thus N will be our symbol for the category "noun."

[7] Grammarians are often accused of using either totally drab or otherwise totally unlikely sentences to illustrate their points. We shall attempt to escape both charges.

[8] Throughout this work we shall follow the convention of calling a noun or pronoun which does not occur as a constituent inside a larger noun phrase itself a noun phrase, and a verb which is not part of a larger verb phrase itself a verb phrase. This convention enables us to say, for example, that every declarative sentence in English consists of an NP and a VP, even when the sentence is only two words long, for example:

(i) Mother called.

for a moment on the relationship of this clause to the verb *to realize*, we perceive that it functions as what is usually called the DIRECT OBJECT of that verb; notice that sentence 2.19 is a possible answer to a question such as:

2.20 What do few congressmen seem to realize?

Since direct objects that are not clauses are invariably NP's (see footnote 8), we may hazard the guess that these clauses, such as the one we have found in 2.19, are NP's too.[9] The clause under consideration may be broken down further into an introductory subordinating conjunction *that*, an NP *the administration's present foreign policy*, and a VP *is leading . . . with China.* This NP may be broken into a variety of constituents, one being the noun *policy*, which is understood to be the HEAD, or main constituent, of the NP. The VP is understood as being made up of a complex verbal expression *is leading*, an NP *our country*, and a PREPOSITIONAL PHRASE (PP) consisting of a PREPOSITION (P) *toward* and an NP *an ultimate . . . with China.* The expression *is leading* is composed of two verbs, *is* and *leading;* fluent speakers furthermore are either aware of, or can be made aware of, some kind of relationship between *is* and the suffix *-ing* of *leading. The country* is made up of the article *the* and a noun *country*, which is its head, while the noun phrase *an ultimate direct confrontation with China* has as its head the noun *confrontation.* This noun has among its *modifiers* a PP *with China*, made up of the preposition *with* and the NP *China*. There is also a relationship between the noun *confrontation* and the verb *confront*, and this relationship is apparent to speakers of English. Some may even point out that the same or similar constituents that can occur with the noun *confrontation* in noun phrases can also occur with the verb *confront* in full sentences, for example:

2.21 Our country will ultimately be directly confronted with China.

The analysis of sentence 2.19 into its constituents may be called its PARSING; what we are claiming is that English speakers' grammatical intuitions include the ability to parse sentences, or at least to recognize and give assent to correct parsings of sentences. The parsing of sentence 2.19 which we undertook in the preceding paragraph can be represented for clarity in diagrammatic form, as in Fig. 2.1. The diagram of Fig. 2.1 may be called, for obvious reasons, a TREE DIAGRAM. We have included in

---

[9]The same observations can be made about subjects as well. A sentence which has a clause as a subject is the following:

(i) That the president of the ladies' auxiliary is really bald comes as no surprise to many people.

the diagram of Fig. 2.1 part-of-speech assignments for all of the words of sentence 2.19, having made for the present an arbitrary decision in the doubtful cases. Moreover, we have represented the SUBORDINATE CLAUSE in that sentence as receiving both the categorization NP and the categorization S (see footnote 8).

As indicated above, judgments about the membership of words in part-of-speech categories, and of the relations of the constituents of sentences to one another as revealed by parsing, represent the simplest kinds of judgments that can be elicited from fluent speakers of the language. Indeed much subtler and more sophisticated judgments concerning the internal structure of sentences are easily elicited from untutored speakers. Such persons, for example, do not require philosophical training in order to perceive that the NP *the Pope* in the following two sentences is being used in two different ways:

>   **2.22**   Bobby wants to be the Pope.
>   **2.23**   Bobby wants to meet the Pope.

In 2.22, *the Pope* refers to the office or position, while in 2.23 *the Pope* refers to the person holding that office. As another illustration, consider the fact that in a sentence such as:

>   **2.24**   He said that Frank went to the movies last
> night.

the PRONOUN *he* cannot refer to the person named *Frank* that occurs after it in the sentence, whereas in:

>   **2.25**   After he went to the movies last night, Frank
> drove 150 miles to visit his former college roommate.

he can refer to the person named *Frank*. Again it is not difficult to elicit such judgments from fluent speakers of English.

Furthermore, it is possible to obtain consistent judgments as to the potential AMBIGUITY of grammatical sentences of English. Not everyone will perceive the ambiguity of such sentences as the following at first sight:

>   **2.26**   The boss fired the salesman with enthusiasm.
>   **2.27**   The scriptwriter was promoted for his enter-
> taining new ideas.
>   **2.28**   Several husky teenagers rolled up the carpet.
>   **2.29**   Ralph took my picture.

But no one will deny their ambiguity once their various interpretations have been pointed out. Thus, the three senses of 2.26 are paraphrasable as:

>   **2.30**   The boss dismissed the salesman from his job
> in an enthusiastic manner.

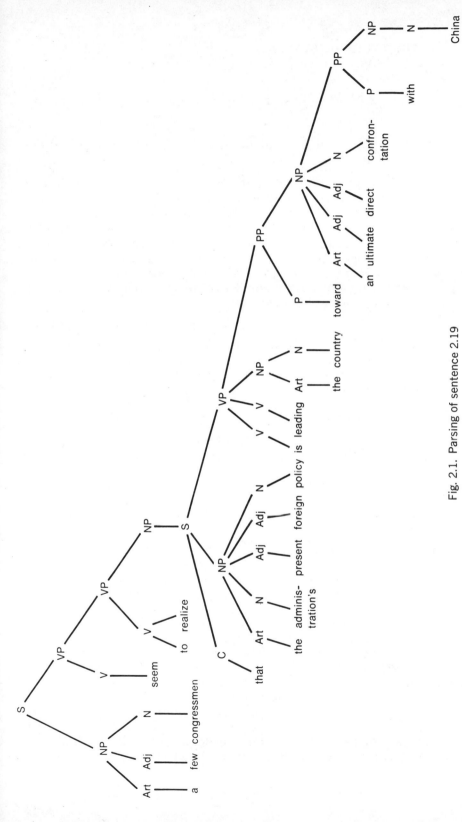

Fig. 2.1. Parsing of sentence 2.19

as:

2.31 The boss instilled enthusiasm in the salesman.

and as:

2.32 The boss dismissed the salesman who had enthusiasm.

The two interpretations of sentence 2.27 depend upon whether one takes *entertaining* or *ideas* as the object of the preposition *for*. Under the former interpretation, *entertaining* is understood as a nominal form related to the verb *entertain* and meaning roughly "considering," with *new ideas* as its object. *Entertaining* in the second case is an adjectival form related to the verb *entertain* and meaning roughly "bringing enjoyment." In 2.28, either *rolled up* can be considered to be the verb, in which case the sentence is paraphrasable as:

2.33 Several husky teenagers rolled the carpet up.

or the verb may be taken to be *roll*, with *up* understood as a preposition, having the following noun phrase as its object, in which case the sentence is not paraphrasable as 2.33. Finally, 2.29 is interpretable in a wide variety of ways; each of the following may be taken as a paraphrase of one specific possible interpretation of the sentence:

2.34 Ralph photographed me.
2.35 Ralph photographed the picture belonging to me.
2.36 Ralph made off with the pictorial representation of me.
2.37 Ralph made off with the picture belonging to me.

Quite obviously, if people are capable of giving assent to the various interpretations of ambiguous sentences such as 2.26–2.29, they must have some means of representing these interpretations of such sentences in their minds. These too are grammatical intuitions.

In certain cases, linguistic intuitions involve the apprehension of grammatical relationships which are not expressed in the overt form of sentences. There seem to be two levels at which certain sentences, at least, are represented: a SURFACE LEVEL corresponding to the overt, physical form of such sentences, and a DEEP LEVEL at which relationships hold which need not hold at the surface level. In the case of ambiguous sentences, such as 2.26–2.29, we may suppose that each interpretation represents a unique set of relationships on the deep level, all of which correspond to a particular representation at the surface level.

A particularly striking class of sentences in which grammatical relationships on the deep level are different from those on the surface level consists of IMPERATIVE sentences, sentences which express commands. On the surface, such sentences as:

2.38 Take these clothes to the laundry.

lack a subject, but on the deep level they possess the subject *you*. In other sentences, what appears as the subject of the sentence on the surface is not the subject on the deep level. Thus although the surface subject of the sentence:

2.39 I began to wonder whether anyone was interested in me.

is the pronoun *I*, on the deep level the subject of the verb *began* is the entire sentence minus the verb *began*, namely *I . . . to wonder whether anyone was interested in me.*[10] By the same token, the NP which appears as the direct object of the verb in a large variety of sentences is not the deep-level direct object. A good illustration of this is provided by the sentence:

2.40 The general expects the enemy machine-gun nest to be wiped out by nightfall.

In this sentence the NP *the enemy machine-gun nest* is the surface direct object but not the deep direct object of *expects*. The latter is in fact everything that follows the verb, namely *the enemy machine-gun nest to be wiped out by nightfall.*

Our linguistic intuitions also enable us to restore constituents which, as a result of what grammarians call ELLIPSIS, do not appear in surface manifestations. Thus in the sentence:

2.41 The woman put her pocketbook in the front seat and her groceries in the back seat.

we understand that *the woman put* has been elided after the conjunction *and;* this intuition enables us to understand sentence 2.41 as having the same meaning as 2.42, in which this ellipsis has not been performed:

2.42 The woman put her pocketbook in the front seat, and she put her groceries in the back seat.

We could go on at considerable length to elaborate the kinds of knowledge that every speaker of a language has in the form of linguistic intuitions about his language. We shall, in fact, con-

---

[10] A similar observation can also be made about sentence 2.19. While the surface-structure subject is indeed *a few congressmen*, the deep-level subject is the entire sentence minus the verb *seem*. Notice also that while on the surface the verb *to realize* has no subject, it can be said to have the deep-level subject *a few congressmen*.

tinue to do so for English in the following chapters. The point is that it is precisely the totality of the knowledge of the language possessed by a fluent speaker that it is incumbent upon a grammarian to describe. The handful of illustrations just given have provided the reader with some appreciation of the magnitude of the job which the grammarian faces. There is a wealth of information to be collected and then systematized, no matter whether one chooses to look at a small handful of selected sentences sharing many structural properties and attempts to describe their structures in detail, or tries to get an overview of the entire language by studying in somewhat less detail the properties of very diverse sentences. Each of these approaches has a place in the study of syntax. The first, which may be called the INTENSIVE approach, is necessary so that we may have available to us the fine details of linguistic structure that are easy to miss when language is looked at superficially, while the second, which may be called the EXTENSIVE approach, is needed so that we do not "miss the forest for the trees." Both of these approaches will be employed in the following chapters. We begin, almost of necessity, with the intensive approach, but after a while we shall find ourselves switching back and forth between these two approaches as we go along.

3 TOWARD A SYNTACTIC DESCRIPTION OF ENGLISH

A syntactic description of a particular language L may be said to be adequate if it accounts for the intuitions of grammaticality held by fluent speakers of L. That is, if a particular linguistic object S is judged by fluent speakers of L to be a sentence of L, then the syntactic description of L must be such that it can tell us that fact; similarly if S is judged to be internally contradictory or ungrammatical in L, then the description must be able to inform us of this fact. Furthermore, for each grammatical sentence of L, the description must indicate the structural properties of that sentence that can be brought to the attention of fluent speakers. We may also wish to require that the description inform us of the nature of the internal contradiction in internally contradictory sentences, and the reasons for the ungrammaticality of ungrammatical objects. To summarize these requirements, it is convenient to think of the syntactic description of L as a BLACK BOX, which receives linguistic objects as input, and produces statements as to the grammaticality and structure of those objects as output, as shown in Fig. 3.1.

As we noted in Chapter 2, speakers of a particular language have subconscious knowledge of the full syntactic description of that language; in other words, the syntactic description of a language which the grammarian seeks to obtain is a model of the capacity of individuals to use (both in speaking and in listening, in writing and in reading) the languages they know, which in turn is the basis for their linguistic intuitions. Now, if we assume that people have subconscious knowledge of full syntactic descriptions of the languages they comprehend, it is reasonable to inquire as to how these descriptions get there. Basically this is a question of developmental psychology, and it

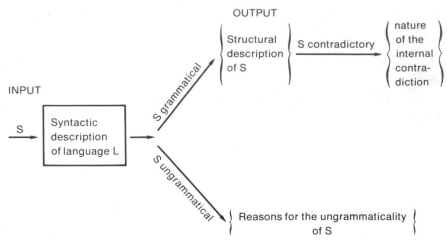

Fig. 3.1. Syntactic description of a language *L* as a "black box."

is a question to which there are yet no firm answers; therefore, we must be content to give merely a rough schematic outline of what seems to happen when a child acquires his native language. We assert as a fundamental principle that children are biologically disposed to acquire a language (see Lenneberg [1967]), and there are at least three reasons that lead us to hold this principle. First, since the acquired capacity is so complex,[1] all of it could not possibly be learned in a lifetime unless the human organism is assumed to have a head start. Second, despite the vastly different experience of each child from that of every other child within the same dialect area as far as exposure to speech is concerned, children learn essentially the same dialect as that of the adults to which they are exposed. Third, the amount of time required for a child to acquire fluency in a language is startlingly brief; children are generally fluent by the age of four. We may elaborate our fundamental principle by saying that each child is equipped with certain expectations about the structure of human language which enable him to perceive the linguistic structures underlying the speech to which he is exposed during infancy and early childhood. Clearly, these expectations must be related to the structural properties that all languages have in common, those a child will not have to learn at all. We may also expect that a child will experience greatest difficulty in acquiring the highly idiosyncratic structural properties of his language. We shall not be concerned further in this book with the problem

---

[1] The reader should realize that the material presented in Chapter 2 represents only a very small fraction of the amount of information available to fluent speakers of English about their language.

of accounting for language acquisition; for further discussion see Chomsky (1965, pp. 47–54); McNeill (1965); and Slobin (1965).

Let us now consider in more detail the properties that a syntactic description of a language must have. Notice first of all that since there is no limit to the number of grammatical sentences in any language, there is no limit to the number of sentences for which a syntactic description must provide a structural description. This means that the description cannot merely amount to a list of the grammatical sentences together with their structural properties; such a list would be infinite, and hence inappropriate as a mòdel of human linguistic capacity. The way in which long and complex sentences are formed, however, provides a helpful clue as to the form which a syntactic description should take. Long and complex sentences invariably contain more simple sentences within them as parts; or to put it more simply, big sentences are made up out of little ones. Furthermore, these simpler sentences function as constituents of the sentences in which they are contained. Thus we saw, for example, that the subordinate clause in sentence 2.19 plays the role of the direct object of a verb. A less complicated example is provided by the subordinate clause of sentence 3.1:

3.1   Politicians know voters prefer results.

If we undertake to parse sentence 3.1 as we parsed 2.19 in the preceding chapter, we come up with a result that can be diagramed as in Fig. 3.2. Furthermore, it would appear that the parsing of sentence 3.1 contains a representation of most of the grammatical intuitions that native speakers have about this

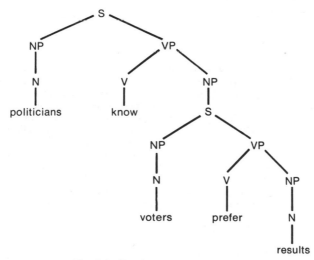

Fig. 3.2. Parsing of sentence 3.1.

sentence; in particular there do not seem to be any deep-level structural properties in sentence 3.1 that are not indicated in Fig. 3.2.[2] Therefore, one of the tasks of a syntactic description of English is to associate the representation of the structure of sentence 3.1, given in Fig. 3.2, with the sentence.

The syntactic description can most simply fulfill this task if it is assumed that it is made up of RULES OF CONSTITUENT MEMBERSHIP. Notice, for example, that in both places where the category S appears in Fig. 3.2, the categories NP and VP occur, in that order, as constituents of S. Similarly, each occurrence of the category VP is made up of the categories V and NP, in that order, while each occurrence of the category NP is made up of either the category N or S. This means that there are rules of English grammar to the following effect: that a sentence may be made up of a noun phrase followed by a verb phrase; that a verb phrase may be made up of a verb followed by a noun phrase; and that a noun phrase may be composed of a noun or of a sentence. Furthermore, the lexical items (words) *politicians, voters,* and *results* are nouns, while *know* and *prefer* are verbs.

We can now state these rules in the notation that has become standard among many contemporary grammarians.[3] If a grammatical category A is allowed to have as its constituents the categories B and C, then we state that rule as follows:

3.2 $A \rightarrow B\ C$

If a grammatical category D has as its constituent the lexical item *a*, then we state that rule as:

3.3 $D \rightarrow a$

In this notation, the rules isolated in the preceding paragraph can be stated as follows:

---

[2] This is as good a time as any to warn the reader that when it comes to syntactic structure, appearances are almost always deceiving; he should never be surprised to find that sentences which on first sight seem to have totally transparent and relatively uninteresting structures turn out upon closer examination to have structures at a deep level which are quite unlike those on the surface. Thus, although we are maintaining, for purposes of this chapter, that the surface structure (parsing) of sentence 3.1 adequately represents all the syntactic properties of the sentence, we will later show that this is not at all the case. The reader should not allow himself to be upset by this fact. The claim that Fig. 3.2 represents the total syntactic structure of sentence 3.1 is to be taken as a *first approximation to the truth* about the structure of the sentences. Later we will introduce closer and closer approximations to the truth — although we will never claim to have arrived at *the whole* truth (no one yet has — for any sentence of any language). We will follow the procedure throughout this book of attempting to systematically arrive closer and closer to the truth about the structure of a wide variety of sentences in English.

[3] The notation is due to Chomsky; it came into widespread use soon after the publication of his work (1957). See pp. 26–27 of that work.

3.4 (a) S → NP VP
      (b) NP → N
      (c) NP → S
      (d) VP → V NP
      (e) N → politicians, voters, results
      (f) V → know, prefer

The rules of 3.4, then, can be considered to be the rules of a grammatical description which assigns the structure given in Fig. 3.2 to sentence 3.1; in short, it *is* such a grammatical description.[4] In general we say that a grammar GENERATES the linguistic objects to which it assigns structural descriptions, and those objects are said to be GRAMMATICAL (alternatively, we say that those objects are sentences) with respect to that grammar. On the other hand, linguistic objects to which the grammar is incapable of assigning a structural description are said to be UNGRAMMATICAL with respect to that grammar. Grammaticality is thus always defined with respect to a particular grammar. Finally, we define the LANGUAGE GENERATED BY A GRAMMAR as all the sentences which it generates.

If we now re-examine grammar 3.4 carefully, we find that it characterizes an infinite number of linguistic objects as grammatical, for the language it generates contains at least one sentence containing 0, 1, 2, 3, . . . subordinate clauses. Thus, besides generating sentence 3.1, with one subordinate clause, grammar 3.4 also generates the following sentences:

      3.5 Voters prefer politicians.

with no subordinate clauses;

      3.6 Politicians know voters know politicians prefer results.

with two subordinate clauses;

      3.7 Voters know politicians know voters know politicians prefer results.

with three subordinate clauses, and so forth. Of course, because of the limited vocabulary contained in 3.4, these more elaborate sentences generated by the grammar are stylistically bad; but if we broaden the vocabulary and yet retain the same grammatical pattern, such sentences make for perfectly acceptable style:

      3.8 Bill is under the impression Harry still believes ministers nowadays preach drinking is sinful.

---

[4] We shall henceforth refer to 3.4 as a grammar, and shall similarly designate all collections of rules which assign structural descriptions to sentences.

Quite obviously, the overwhelming majority of English sentences are ungrammatical with respect to grammar 3.4—for example, every sentence containing at least one English word not in the vocabulary of 3.4—and it even fails to generate certain grammatical English sentences made up entirely of words in its vocabulary such as:

3.9 Voters politicians know prefer results.

On the other hand, grammar 3.4 generates certain sentences which are internally contradictory without telling us why they are. For example, it generates the sentence:

3.10 Results prefer politicians.

without informing us that it is contradictory because the verb *prefer* requires that its subject be ANIMATE while the subject noun phrase *results* is in fact INANIMATE. A more serious shortcoming of grammar 3.4 when viewed as a start toward a total syntactic description of English is that it assigns more than one structural description to every sentence it generates having more than one subordinate clause. Thus, to take sentence 3.1 as an example, besides assigning it the structural description diagramed in Fig. 3.2, this grammar also assigns it the following description, which, quite obviously, it is not felt to have in English:

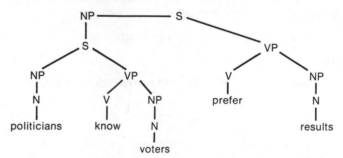

Fig. 3.3. Incorrect structure assigned to sentence 3.1 by grammar 3.4.

Sentence 3.6, besides being assigned the structure it has in English, is also assigned three other structural descriptions by grammar 3.4, none of which it is felt to have in English.

Let us now examine how it is that grammar 3.4 assigns these unwanted structural descriptions. The basic reason is that rule 3.4(c), which permits an NP to consist of an S, in particular permits a subject NP to consist of an S. Now, as we observed in Chapter 2, footnote 10, subordinate clauses can function as subjects of English sentences, but when they do, they must of necessity be introduced by some subordinating conjunction such as *that*.[5] Even so, such noun phrases are not typically used as subjects of such verbs as *know* and *prefer*. The following examples are internally contradictory, just like example 3.10:

3.11 That politicians prefer results knows voters.
3.12 That voters know politicians prefers results.

Such grammatical facts as the internal contradictory character of 3.10–3.12 and the restrictions on the occurrence of the subordinating conjunction *that* cannot be readily represented by rules having the form of 3.2 and 3.3. We can think of grammars containing rules just of that configuration as forming the basis for the parsing of sentences into constituents.[6] To the extent that such parsing reveals true grammatical properties of sentences of languages such as English, grammars having that form are adequate for the description of syntactic structure. To the extent that such parsing fails to do so (and we have presented some evidence in Chapter 2 and in the present chapter that such is the case), then either rules of that form should be gotten rid of altogether and replaced by rules having in and of themselves the power to describe all syntactic structure; or rules of that form do play a role in a grammar of a language, but they need to be supplemented by rules having a different form.

The evidence presented in Chapter 2 would appear to favor the second alternative. There we showed that although many sentences have syntactic properties not evident upon simple parsing into constituents, the deep-level structural properties of those sentences (properties that do not show up under parsing) *are* describable in terms of rules of the form 3.2 and 3.3. It turns out that all deep-level structural relationships are themselves statable in terms of constituent structure. For example, when we

---

[5] Notice that subordinate clauses which function as direct objects may, but do not have to, be introduced by *that*. The presence or absence of this word has no effect on the meaning of the entire sentence. Thus the following sentence has the same meaning as that of example 3.1:

    (i) Politicians know that voters prefer results.

Facts such as this about English shall concern us further in Chapter 5.

[6] Rules of the form 3.2 and 3.3 are known technically as CONTEXT-FREE CONSTITUENT (or PHRASE) STRUCTURE rules; henceforth we shall designate them simply as CONSTITUENT-STRUCTURE RULES. Grammars made up entirely of constituent-structure rules are known as CONSTITUENT-STRUCTURE GRAMMARS; languages generated (see footnote 7) by such grammars are known as CONSTITUENT-STRUCTURE LANGUAGES. For further elementary discussion, see Bach (1964), Langendoen (1969). The study of grammars in terms of the form of their rules is now a fairly well-developed mathematical subspecialty which students with background in modern algebra might enjoy looking into further. The field as it had developed up to 1963 is thoroughly covered in the three chapters by Chomsky and Miller in Luce, Bush, and Galanter (1963). More recent developments are contained mainly in the journals *Information and Control* and the *Journal of the Association for Computing Machinery*, and in Ginsburg (1966).

examined sentence 2.38, we stated that at the deep level of analysis, this sentence has a subject and a predicate, but that this subject and predicate are different from the surface-level subject and predicate of the sentence. Sentence 2.40, we observed, at the deep level contains constituents missing from the surface-level representation; when we "restore" those constituents, we observe that rules of the form 3.2 and 3.3 are adequate to characterize the structure of the sentence at the deep level.

We say then that the deep-level structure (henceforth we shall simply refer to this as DEEP STRUCTURE) of sentences of languages such as English is describable in terms of rules having the form 3.2 and 3.3. The surface-level structure (henceforth SURFACE STRUCTURE) of sentences is obtained from deep structures by means of rules which rearrange or delete the constituents appearing in deep structures. Such rules, which have the property of rearranging and/or deleting constituents, will be given the name GRAMMATICAL TRANSFORMATIONS, or simply, TRANSFORMATIONS. The properties of such rules will be taken up in Chapter 5.[7]

Before going on to consider other constituent-structure rules which are required for a description of English [other than rules 3.4(a–d), that is], we shall give one more example to substantiate the claims made in the foregoing two paragraphs. Consider first the sentence cited in Chapter 2, footnote 10, which we repeat here for convenience:

3.13 That the president of the ladies' auxiliary is really bald comes as no surprise to many people.

and the following sentence:

3.14 It comes as no surprise to many people that the president of the ladies' auxiliary is really bald.

These two sentences do not differ in meaning; they represent two different ways of saying exactly the same thing, although everyone will probably agree that example 3.13 is somewhat more "formal." In both sentences, we would want to say the deep-structure subject is the subordinate clause *that the president . . . bald*, but this clause is the surface-structure subject only of 3.13. In 3.14, we would like to say, the deep-structure subject has been moved out of subject position, leaving behind the pro-

---

[7] The label "generative-transformational" appearing in the subtitle of this book is obtained from two different characteristics of the conception of the grammar under discussion. Such grammars are "generative" in that they are intended to supply structural descriptions for all linguistic objects which are grammatical in particular languages; they are "transformational" in that they contain grammatical transformations which relate deep structures to surface structures. The term "transformational-generative" is also used.

noun *it*,[8] and put at the end of the entire sentence. We do say precisely this if we maintain there is a transformational rule in English grammar which performs the operation of thus trans-posing a subordinate clause functioning as a noun phrase, under certain conditions, leaving behind a pronoun in the vacated spot. We can even give a name to the rule — EXTRAPOSITION — a name devised by the great Danish grammarian Otto Jespersen (1937). Jespersen's account was of course not generative-transforma-tional, and upon examining his work it is not entirely clear which syntactic phenomena he wished to call extraposition and which APPOSITION. As we shall see later on, these two phenomena are quite different. The definitive generative-transformational account of extraposition in English to date is by Rosenbaum (1967). We shall take up in Chapter 5 the problem of describing the extraposition transformation, what it does, and the condi-tions under which it may apply.

We now consider what other constituent-structure rules are required for English. Since almost every claim about what these rules are [including rules 3.4(a–d)] can be seriously challenged, we shall limit our discussion to a few rules which can at least be defended as not wholly unreasonable.

Rule 3.4(d) permits a verb phrase to consist of a verb and a noun phrase; but we shall need another rule in light of the fol-lowing examples:

3.15 An untimely arrest took place.
3.16 Last Tuesday, in the vicinity of War Zone D, an entire platoon of American soldiers vanished.
3.17 Several minutes went by while the sound crew unsuccessfully attempted to get the microphone to operate.

The other rule we need is this:

3.18 VP → V

Traditionally, we apply the label INTRANSITIVE to verbs which occur by themselves within verb phrases; verbs which occur with a following noun phrase as object are called TRANSITIVE verbs. In 3.15–3.17 the intransitive verbs *took place, vanished, went by* appear.[9] (It might be objected that *took place* cannot be called an intransitive verb at all, since it is two words — a verb *took* and a noun *place*. Observe, however, that *took place* in sentence 3.15

---

[8] In Chapter 5 we will more precisely define what it means to say that a rule has "left be-hind" a pronoun.

[9] More precisely we should say that the past-tense forms of the verbs *take place, vanish*, and *go by* appear in these sentences. For discussion of the relation between past-tense forms of verbs and their "lexical representations," see Chapter 7.

is a fixed lexical expression whose significance is unrelated to that of the independently occurring verb *took* or noun *place*. Furthermore, the expression functions exactly as does the indubitably intransitive verbs *occur, happen*, and so forth. Consequently, we shall have to admit to the English lexicon items that are themselves composed of lexical items. This matter is discussed further in Chapter 4.)

However, while it may at first seem clear that there are transitive and intransitive verbs in English (for example, *know, prefer, hit* and *take place, vanish, go by*, respectively), and that hence rules 3.4(d) and 3.18 are required for English, we shall see that upon closer examination it is by no means clear that the distinction is required.[10] In addition we must call into question the deep-level validity of the distinction between subject and predicate, that is the deep-level validity of rule 3.4(a).

The skepticism expressed in the preceding paragraph can be summarized as follows: While it is clear that in the surface structures of many English sentences one can distinguish NP's functioning as subjects and as objects of V's, it is not clear that the deep-level relationship between NP's and V's is that of subject-of and object-of. One reason for this is that the same noun phrase can function as both subject and object of the same verb, with no change in the deep-level relationship between the verb and the noun phrase. The following examples illustrate this point:

3.19 The tree shook.
3.20 The boy shook the tree.

Whatever the deep level relationship is between the NP *the tree* and the V *shook*, it is the same relationship whether the NP is the surface-level subject, as in 3.19, or the surface-level object, as in 3.20. Conversely, the deep-level relationship between the NP *the boy* and the V *shook* is different in sentence 3.20 from what it is in 3.21:

3.21 The boy shook.

despite the fact that in both sentences, *the boy* is the surface subject of the verb. Of course, as the reader has probably already realized, the verb *shook* in 3.19 is different in meaning from *shook* in 3.20. In the latter sentence, *shook the tree* can be replaced by *caused the tree to shake*, with no significant change in the meaning of the sentence. In 3.20, the NP *the tree* can be said to be the

---

[10] Recall that when we say this, we are talking about syntactic relationships at the deep level, not the surface level. On the surface level the distinction is quite clear, but that fact is irrelevant to the problem of determining deep-level syntactic relationships.

PATIENT (that which undergoes shaking) of the sentence—similarly *the boy* in 3.21.

A somewhat different situation is presented by the following sentences:

3.22 The metal dissolved.

3.23 The innocent-looking acid dissolved the metal.

At first glance, 3.22 and 3.23 seem parallel in structure to sentences 3.19 and 3.20, the only significant difference being that the surface-level subject of 3.23 does not designate an animate being. But the difference goes deeper than that. In 3.23, we understand that acid to be either that *in* which the metal dissolved or that *with* which the metal was dissolved; that is to say, sentence 3.23 is actually ambiguous. The first interpretation is paraphrased by the sentence:

3.24 The metal dissolved in the innocent-looking acid.

The second interpretation is not so directly paraphrasable. It implies the existence of an animate *agent* who used the acid to dissolve the metal. If we specify such an agent, we may obtain:

3.25 The chemist dissolved the metal with the innocent-looking acid.

In summary, we say that wherever the various NP's are used in these sentences, *the metal* is the patient, *the chemist* is the agent, and *the innocent-looking acid* is either the location or the instrument. In 3.24, the locative relation is made explicit by means of the preposition *in*, and in 3.25 the instrumental relation is indicated by the preposition *with*. In 3.23, where no preposition is used, both relations are possible.

This leads directly to the second problem, namely that in English the significant relationship of noun phrases to verbs is often but not always indicated by a preposition. Consider the following sentence:

3.26 Harvey arrived at the airport just in time to catch the plane to New York.

Here *the airport* stands in a locative relationship to the verb *arrived,* as is indicated by the presence of *at.* However, in the sentence:

3.27 Harvey reached the airport just in time to catch the plane to New York.

no overt indication is given that *the airport* stands in the same relationship to the verb *reached.* Now, we are accustomed to think of *the airport* as the (surface level) direct object of *reached* in 3.27 and in sentences like it, whereas in 3.27 we consider *at the airport* to be a (surface level) adverbial of location. But at the level of deep structure the relationships are identical, and they should be so represented. Either both expressions are direct objects in deep structure or neither is; in any event, the significant relationship is one of location.

Similar problems arise when we attempt to deal with the deep structural relationships between adjectives and noun phrases in English sentences. One of the more significant observations to come out of recent generative-transformational research in English syntax is that adjectives and verbs share many properties in common (Lakoff [1965]); adjectives merely have the special characteristic that at the surface level, at least, they are preceded by a form of the verb *be*, and that if an NP follows them, a preposition is required to go with it. Thus the adjective *happy* and the verb *rejoice* differ only in that the former must be preceded by a form of *be:*

>**3.28** The man was happy to learn that he was the new father of twin boys.
>**3.29** The man rejoiced to learn that he was the new father of twin boys.

But the verb *fear* and the adjective *afraid* differ not only in this respect, but also in that the object of *afraid* must be preceded by the preposition *of:*

>**3.30** Our little chihuahua doesn't fear strangers.
>**3.31** Our little chihuahua isn't afraid of strangers.

Similarly, *frighten* and *frightening* differ in that the NP following *frightening* must be introduced by *to:*

>**3.32** Strangers frightened our little chihuahua.
>**3.33** Strangers were frightening to our little chihuahua.

From examples 3.30–3.33, moreover, we can also see that the significant relationships between an adjective and a noun phrase do not correspond simply with whether those NP's are subject or object of the adjective at the surface level. Whatever the relationships that the NP's *strangers* and *our little chihuahua* bear to the adjectives *afraid* and *frightening*, they are the same relationships in both cases.[11]

We see that when we attempt to establish the validity of very simple constituent-structure rules governing the relationships

---

[11] We leave as a problem to be dealt with later (Chapter 6) why sentence 3.32 is ambiguous whereas 3.33 is not.

between verbs and adjectives and noun phrases, we run into a host of difficulties. Let us see if we can deal with the problem of the internal constituent structure of noun phrases. So far, we have two very simple rules, 3.4(b-c), which state that noun phrases may be made up of a single constituent, either a noun or a sentence. Clearly, in English, however, a noun phrase can have a much more complicated internal structure. For example, an NP in English can consist of an N followed by an S; the subject of the following sentence is an illustration:

> **3.34** People who live in glass houses shouldn't throw stones.

The subordinate clause *who live in glass houses* in sentence 3.34 is known as a RELATIVE CLAUSE. The element *who*, which introduces it, is called a RELATIVE PRONOUN; it refers to the same thing as the head noun of the NP, *people*. Hence we say that *people* is the ANTECEDENT of the relative pronoun. In 3.34 *who* functions as the subject of the verb in the relative clause. The relative pronoun, may, however, stand for the object of the verb (in which case it is either *who* or *whom*, the latter being the preferred form for many speakers of English) or in fact, within certain limits, for any noun phrase in the relative clause. Furthermore, if the antecedent is inanimate, the relative pronoun is *which* rather than *who* or *whom* and in certain special cases the relative pronoun may take the form *whose, when, where,* or *why*. In addition, the form *that* may be used as a relative pronoun. The following illustrate some of the various possibilities:

> **3.35** The man who(m) I saw running out of the bank turned out to have been the thief who robbed it.
> **3.36** I am the man whose coat you took last night by mistake.
> **3.37** You can do it any time when it is convenient for you.
> **3.38** This is the town where we were arrested last spring for parading without a permit.
> **3.39** No one knows the reason why we are here.
> **3.40** I have a watch which needs repair.

To accommodate these facts within a syntactic description, suppose we formulate as a constituent-structure rule of English the following:

> **3.41** NP → N S

with the stipulation that the relative clause (the S on the right-hand side of the rule 3.4) contains an NP which consists of the N which is modified by the relative clause. Then, by a transformational rule (which we shall discuss in Chapter 5), this N is replaced by a relative pronoun of the appropriate form, which is also moved to the front of the relative clause.

In Chapter 5, we shall also discuss a transformational rule which deletes the relative pronoun *who* or *which* and any form of the verb *be* when they occur together. This rule is needed to account for the fact, among others, that the following pairs of sentences are felt to have the same deep structure:

3.42 Margie wears clothes which are attractive to men.
3.43 Margie wears clothes attractive to men.

Notice, however, that when what is left ends with an adjective after this transformation is applied, another transformational rule applies to move that adjective to a position preceding the modified noun. Thus we have:

3.44 Margie wears clothes which are attractive.
3.45 Margie wears attractive clothes.

whereas the following is *E*-ungrammatical:

3.46 *Margie wears clothes attractive.

This last transformation does not apply, however, if the modified noun is an indefinite pronoun such as *someone* (compare examples 2.15-2.16).

Certain nouns are capable of occurring with another noun phrase; such nouns can be thought of as being analogous to transitive verbs. Such nouns include, among others, kinship terms such as *brother, daughter, uncle, wife;* body parts such as *face, mouth, heart, hand;* certain occupational terms such as *aide, secretary;* and spatial terms such as *top, right, side.* The noun phrase occurring with such a noun is either introduced by a preposition such as *of, to,* as in:

3.47 The lumberjack lopped off the top of the tree.
3.48 Susie was appointed secretary to the president of the company.

or it is inflected with the GENITIVE CASE marker *'s* as in:

3.49 The principal's daughter eloped with John's cousin's fiance.

Ignoring again the problem presented by the prepositions, and the problem of getting the surface-structure word order correct, let us assume that there is the following constituent-structure rule in English:

3.50 NP → N NP

This completes for now our consideration of the constituent-structure rules governing the internal structure of noun and verb phrases. The reader should be aware of both the great number of considerations concerning the constituent structure of sentences that we have not even begun to deal with and of the problematic status of the rules we have formulated. We conclude this chapter with a consideration of the phenomenon of coordination, particularly that of sentences.

We observed earlier that long, complex sentences in English are made up of smaller sentences. In all the examples we have considered thus far in this chapter, these smaller sentences have played a subordinate role in the sentence as a whole, either as a noun phrase or as a relative clause within a noun phrase. However, it is also possible to construct long sentences by connecting simple sentences together using a coordinating conjunction such as *and:*

> **3.51**   My sister is a columnist for the *Daily Worker*, and my brother spies for the Russians, and I make my living by writing original articles for the *Reader's Digest.*

If we designate the conjoined sentences in 3.51 as S_1, S_2, and S_3, respectively, we represent the parsing of that sentence as in Fig. 3.4. Since the number of sentences that can be conjoined in

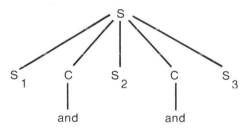

Fig. 3.4.   Parsing of sentence 3.51.

this way is, theoretically at least, unlimited, it is not immediately obvious how to write a constituent-structure rule to permit the generation of compound sentences such as 3.51. It is clearly unsatisfactory to have to postulate an infinity of rules, thus:

> **3.52**   (a) $S \rightarrow S\ C\ S$
> (b) $S \rightarrow S\ C\ S\ C\ S$
> (c) $S \rightarrow S\ C\ S\ C\ S\ C\ S$
> .   .
> .   .
> .   .

What is required is a statement which abbreviates the infinity of rules of the form 3.52; such a statement is known technically as a RULE SCHEMA, and the rule schema that has been devised as an abbreviation for the rules of 3.52 is the following:

3.53 S → C S*

For simplicity of discussion from this point, we will limit our examples of compound sentences to those having exactly two conjoined sentences. When the two conjoined sentences in a compound sentence have identical parts, one occurrence of the identical part is usually deleted (compare example 2.40). This deletion is accomplished by a transformational rule, to be discussed in Chapter 5, known as CONJUNCTION REDUCTION. In particular, when the entire predicates of the two conjoined sentences are identical, the result of conjunction reduction yields a sentence with conjoined noun phrases. Thus if we start out with a deep-level conjunction of sentence:

3.54 President Johnson flew to Guam and Secretary McNamara flew to Guam.

we end up, after conjunction reduction, with surface-level conjunction of NP's:

3.55 President Johnson and Secretary McNamara flew to Guam.

However, there are sentences containing conjoined NP's for which it is not possible to assume that they arose from deep-level sentence conjunction. Consider, for example:

3.56 President Johnson and Secretary McNamara are similar in their outlook on the role of the military in American society.

Sentence 3.56 cannot possibly be thought of as arising from a deep-level conjunction of two sentences, since there are no *E*-grammatical sentences which could possibly serve as CONJUNCTS. The simplest solution is to assume that besides deep-level sentence conjunction in English, we have also deep-level NP conjunction; that is, that there is a rule schema in English as follows:

3.57 NP → C NP*

Matters relating to conjunction will be considered at various points in the following chapters; the relationship between plurality and conjunction in Chapter 4, the transformational rules of conjunction reduction, and further matters relating to the differences between sentence and noun-phrase conjunction, in Chapter 5.

For the convenience of the reader, and for our own convenience in later reference, we shall now state all of the constituent-structure rules for English that we have presented up to this point; the number that the rule had when it was introduced is given in parentheses after the statement of the rule here:

3.58	(a)	$S \rightarrow NP\ VP$	**(3.4a)**
	(b)	$NP \rightarrow N$	**(3.4b)**
	(c)	$NP \rightarrow S$	**(3.4c)**
	(d)	$NP \rightarrow N\ S$	**(3.41)**
	(e)	$NP \rightarrow N\ NP$	**(3.50)**
	(f)	$VP \rightarrow V\ NP$	**(3.4d)**
	(g)	$VP \rightarrow V$	**(3.18)**
	(h)	$S \rightarrow C\ S^{*}$	**(3.53)**
	(i)	$NP \rightarrow C\ NP^{*}$	**(3.57)**

4 THE NATURE OF SEMANTICS

From a consideration of our examples of internally contradictory sentences 2.5–2.10, it is clear that words have certain properties which are expressible only in terms of combinations of more basic elements. This can also be seen from an examination of words in terms of their meanings; for example the word *boy* in one of its senses means a relatively young male human being; conversely, *girl* means a relatively young female human being. The elements relatively young, male, female, human, and so on can be thought of as components, or features, of the meaning of these words, and the meanings of these words may be considered to be built up out of combinations of these features. Very general words, such as *thing, stuff, animal,* and the like, can be thought of as having meanings built up out of relatively few and relatively general features of meaning, or as we shall henceforth call them, SEMANTIC FEATURES. Words having a very specific meaning, such as *midwife, sparrow, wrench,* and so forth can be thought of as being built up out of relatively many and relatively specific semantic features. A word having two or more meanings, a so-called homonym, such as *set, yard, bank,* corresponds to two or more different combinations of semantic features.

The fact that the meanings of words are expressible in terms of more basic elements has been known since antiquity; the assumption of this fact underlies all dictionary construction. What most dictionary-makers fail to make profitable use of, however, is that semantic features are not arbitrary things invented on the spot for the definition of particular words, but that they are systematically a part of the meanings of many words. Lexicographers also fail to make profitable use of the fact that the combination of semantic features in the meanings of words is also systematic; it is not new for each new word under definition.

The first serious attempt to incorporate these ideas, and others, into the generative-transformational framework was by Katz and Fodor (1963). Their work has since stimulated a considerable amount of interest in tackling the very complex problem of getting at the specification of the meanings of words, even among linguists who do not work exclusively within that framework, for example Nida (1964). Considerable criticism has also been generated. See, for example, Bolinger (1965), Weinreich (1963, 1966a), Bendix (1966), Bierwisch (1967 and forthcoming). For Katz's reply to Weinreich (1966a), see Katz (1967).

Actually, Katz and Fodor were attempting to arrive at a semantic characterization, not of words per se, but of entities called LEXICAL ITEMS, which in many instances are words but which in others may be part of a word, or a group of words—for example the expression *take place*, which we saw in Chapter 3 may be considered a single syntactic item. Moreover, they were concerned to determine how the meaning of a sentence could be arrived at by means of rules which amalgamate the individual meanings of its constituents. This problem they called the semantic PROJECTION PROBLEM.[1] For the time being, we need not be concerned with the form of these rules, but it should be noted at this point that the meaning of a sentence is determined by semantic-projection rules operating on its deep structure, not on its surface structure. This enables us to say why it is that sentences which have the same deep structure, for example sentences 3.13 and 3.14, are identical in meaning, and why two sentences with the same pronunciation or written form but with different deep structures (what we have been calling ambiguous sentences) have different meanings.[2]

Since Katz and Fodor's pioneering paper a considerable amount of work has been done on the problem of establishing the properties of, and the interrelations among, the semantic features of natural languages. Some of this work has been completely original, but much, if not most, of it has involved the attempt to clarify and make explicit the work of earlier scholars — going back at least as far as that of Aristotle—on these and related problems. Among the insights gained have been the following: Many semantic features may be termed binary, many are

---

[1] For further discussion, see Katz and Postal (1964) and Katz (1966).

[2] This statement is somewhat of an oversimplification, for it is possible that two sentences with the same meaning will have different deep structures. The opposite possibility, that two sentences with the same deep structure might have different meanings, is the subject of considerable disagreement among linguists; the same is true of the possibility that deep structures do not completely determine the meanings of sentences. We shall take the position here that deep structure specifications do completely determine meanings, but the reader is warned that this is a claim, not a proven fact.

hierarchically related to one another, many others are cross classifying. Let us discuss the nature of these insights in order.[3]

The binary character of certain semantic features is established by the observation that there are many pairs of lexical items whose difference in meaning can be pinpointed to a single difference with respect to some feature. Thus the nouns *boy* and *girl* can be thought of as having meanings which are built up in identical fashion from semantic features, except that in the case of *boy*, the feature of maleness is present, and in the case of *girl*, femaleness. But rather than refer to maleness and femaleness as separate semantic features, we can instead think of them as opposite specifications of a single feature, let us say Masculine. Formally, we may say that basic semantic elements are not semantic features as such, but specifications of semantic features. In the case of binary features, such as Masculine, we can indicate the specification by means of plus and minus signs. Let us say that [+Masculine][4] is the specification found in the semantic representation of nouns such as *boy, man, bull*, while [−Masculine] is that which is present in the representations of nouns such as *girl, woman, cow*. Pairs of words such as *boy* and *girl* can be considered to be ANTONYMOUS as regards the binary feature Masculine.[5] Other binary features that one might wish to establish on the basis of similar relatively simple reflection on the meanings of nouns include Human, Animate, and Abstract.

The semantic representation of individual nouns can be thought of as being made up, in part at least, of combinations of binary feature specifications; thus *boy*, for example, has the specifications [+Human, +Masculine]. On the other hand, *child* is what we may call UNSPECIFIED for the feature Masculine; it may be represented without any sign in front of that feature, thus [+Human, Masculine]. The noun *table*, to take another example, receives the specification [−Animate, −Abstract]; not only is *table* unspecified for the feature Masculine, that feature is inappropriate to its semantic representation. Accordingly, the feature may be left entirely out of account when it comes to the semantic representation of this noun.

This takes us to the second insight: the hierarchical nature of some of the semantic features. A noun which is specified as [+Human] may be automatically considered to have the specifications [+Animate, −Abstract]. The specifications [+Human],

---

[3] Much of what is said in the following discussion is treated in greater detail and with greater attention to formalism by Chomsky (1965, Chapters 2 and 4).

[4] From here on, we will follow the practice of enclosing features together with their specifications within square brackets.

[5] But *not* such pairs as *boy* and *woman*, which differ in more than one feature specification.

[+Animate], [−Abstract] and [+Abstract], [−Animate], [−Human] each form a hierarchy of specificity. A noun which is specified for any term in either hierarchy is automatically specified for every term below it in that hierarchy. We can also characterize the notion of the appropriateness of a feature, such as Masculine, in terms of such hierarchies. This feature is inappropriate for any noun which does not have the feature specification second from the top in the first hierarchy, that is, [+Animate].[6]

On the other hand, consider the relationship between the features Human and Masculine. Specifications for these features are not hierarchically arranged; rather all possible combinations of specifications of these features are found in the semantic representation of various lexical items. Thus the noun *boy* has the specifications [+Human, +Masculine]; *girl* the specifications [+Human, −Masculine]; *bull* the specifications [−Human, +Masculine]; and *cow* the specifications [−Human, −Masculine]. We say that the features Human and Masculine are CROSS CLASSIFYING rather than hierarchic.

Before proceeding further with our investigation of the properties of semantic features and their role in syntactic description, it would be well for us to point out three basic and not entirely unrelated facts about semantic features in general. The first of these has to do with the relationship between semantic features and classes of objects and properties of the physical universe. Quite clearly there is a close relationship between semantic features and the nature of the physical world, but it would be a mistake to identify these features with classes of objects and properties of the physical world. This is true for various reasons; among them is the fact that in any language there are terms for fictitious objects (for example, English *centaur*) which nevertheless are easily definable in terms of combinations of semantic features that are employed elsewhere in the definition of other objects (fictitious or not). Similarly, every language makes provision for the construction of terms by allowing for the combination of semantic-feature specifications in novel ways, such that the term can make reference to objects which cannot even be pictured in the mind, much less found in the real world (for example, English *chiliagon*, meaning a polygon having 1000 sides).

The first fact to be pointed out here, then, is that semantic features do not represent properties of the universe but innate properties of the human mind itself and of the human perceptual apparatus. This is to say that the child, in learning his na-

---

[6] A more careful analysis will reveal that the feature Masculine is in fact inappropriate even for certain animate nouns designating "lower" living organisms, such as *bug*, *worm*, and the like. This detail, however, need not concern us here.

tive language, is predisposed to assign innately given feature specifications to the lexical items he is acquiring; so is the foreigner attempting to learn a new language; so is any adult who is acquiring new terms or redefining previously learned words in terms of new knowledge. Naturally, we do not expect to find that for each lexical item in one language, there is a corresponding item with the same representation in terms of semantic-feature specifications in another language, or that one language will use all the semantic features found in the investigation of the semantic features of all languages. Rather, we mean to say that if a particular semantic feature is found to play a role in a language, the interpretation of that feature will be in terms of the innate properties of the human mind and of human perception.[7]

The second fact that should be observed is that although certain nouns may be unspecified for a certain feature, for example Masculine, the grammar may have a rule which requires it to have a specification for that feature. Thus the personal pronouns which refer to human nouns are *he* and *she*, and they require that their antecedents be [+Masculine] and [−Masculine] respectively. The question arises, then, what pronoun is selected to replace human nouns, such as *cousin, person*, or *someone*, which are unspecified for Masculine? The answer is that the form *he* is used; moreover it is used without committing the speaker as to the gender of the antecedent. Thus in the sentence:

4.1   Someone said that he was sick.

under the interpretation that *he* refers to the same person as *someone*, it is not necessary that the person referred to by *someone* be male.[8] The pronoun *she*, of course, may be used also, but

---

[7] For further discussion, see Bierwisch (1967, pp. 2-4). An interesting observation to be made in this connection is the fact that in many "primitive languages" there are well-developed biological taxonomies that correspond almost exactly with the scientific classification of the species named. This suggests quite strongly that the ability to perceive animals and plants according to their scientific classification is innate in the human mind and develops automatically if the individual is provided with the proper experience of observing other people name things. Now, the scientific classification of biological entities into species is not itself arbitrary, but is in fact a classification of them into populations which will interbreed with each other but not with other populations. Thus the propensity to perceive living things in terms of populations which interbreed with each other is innate in humans. For a discussion of the animal (particularly the bird) taxonomy of the Fore, a New Guinea highland tribe, see Diamond (1966). I am indebted to Professor Leon Warshay for bringing Diamond's article to my attention.

[8] The [+Human] nouns *baby, infant*, and *child* are exceptions to this in that the pronoun which replaces these nouns may be *it*. One can easily think of a variety of possible explanations for this fact—for example, that people feel that when they refer to a baby whose sex they do not know as *he*, and it turns out to be a girl, they have thereby committed a faux pas.

then it is clearly understood that the person referred to is female. We say that the specification [+Masculine] is the UN-MARKED member of the pair of specifications [+Masculine], [−Masculine]; this is to say that whenever a noun which is unspecified for Masculine has to be replaced by a pronoun for which the feature is specified, then the pronoun specified [+Masculine] is used.

The unmarked character of the specification [+Masculine] shows up in English in other ways, as well. In many cases where we have a pair of terms, one referring to the female of the species and the other to the male, the term referring to the male is also used as the name of the species. Examples include *man* (male and species) versus *woman* (female only); *fox* (male and species) versus *vixen* (female); *horse* (male and species) versus *mare* (female only); *tiger* (male and species) versus *tigress* (female only). There are, to be sure, a number of exceptions: *duck* (female and species) versus *drake* (male only); *goose* (female and species) versus *gander* (male only), but these are much fewer. Moreover, as the *tiger* versus *tigress* case shows, it is possible to form certain [−Masculine] nouns by the addition of a suffix to nouns which are either unspecified for Masculine (e.g. *poet*), which are specified as [+Masculine], (e.g. *duke*), or which, like *tiger*, are either unspecified or are specified [+Masculine]. The only case in English that I am aware of in which a suffix is attached to a noun specified as [−Masculine] to render it [+Masculine] is *widow* versus *widower*,[9] and I know of no cases in English in which a suffix is attached to a noun unspecified for Masculine to render it [+Masculine].

The third fact to be noted is that semantic-feature specifications need to be distinguished from grammatical-feature specifications in those languages, such as French and German, in which they go by the same name. Thus in French the noun *femme* is [−Masculine] in two different respects. In one respect it is [−Masculine] for the same reason that the English nouns *woman* and *wife* are [−Masculine]; the specification is part of the meaning of the lexical item. The other respect in which it is [−Masculine] is that it occurs with the definite article *la* instead of *le*, is modified by the feminine form of adjectives such as *belle* instead of *beau*, and so on. On the other hand a noun such as *table* in French is [−Masculine] only in the second of these respects. Like its English cognate, it has no such semantic-feature specifications.

An interesting complication arises in French because there

---

[9] One might venture also *bride* versus *bridegroom* as comparable, but the use of the noun *groom* as a synonym of *bridegroom* indicates quite clearly that this lexical element is not a suffix.

are nouns, such as *professeur* "professor," which are semantically unspecified for Masculine but are grammatically [+Mascu-
line]. Because this specification is also the unmarked semantic
one, everything is fine, until a French speaker wants to say the
French equivalent of:

4.2 The professor is pregnant.

in which clearly a female professor is understood. For obvious
reasons, the adjective *enceinte* "pregnant" only occurs in a
feminine form, but if it is used in the French equivalent of 4.2,
namely:

4.3 Le professeur est enceinte.

then the grammatical rule of agreement of gender between
nouns and adjectives is broken.

Let us return now to the point in our discussion from which
we digressed to state the three facts just mentioned. We have so
far shown, on the basis of fairly elementary considerations, that
the meanings of lexical items are statable, at least in part, in
terms of semantic features, many of which are binary, and whose
specifications relative to one another are either hierarchic or
cross classifying. Let us inquire next whether there are any
semantic features which are not binary One possibility that
suggests itself immediately is Dimensional, simply because
human visual perception is in terms of three dimensions, and it
is reasonable to suppose that these dimensions are independent
of one another. Suppose, then, we posit a semantic feature Dimensional, which takes on the values 1, 2, 3, and possibly also 0.
Thus, the terms of measurement, *length, area,* and *volume,* can
be considered to have the specifications [1 Dimensional], [2 Di-
mensional], and [3 Dimensional], respectively, while objects
may also be classified according to their dimensionality (usually
2 or 3). Thus *profile, circle* are [2 Dimensional] while *room, box,
hole, sphere* are [3 Dimensional]. The only [1 Dimensional]
nouns are concepts such as *line, radius, tangent,* while *point* is
classifiable, conceptually at least, as [0 Dimensional].

The penetrability of objects suggests a feature Penetrable,
again with values of 1, 2, and 3, where we take *gas* to have the
specification [1 Penetrable], *liquid* [2 Penetrable], and *solid*
[3 Penetrable]. In the case of the chemical compound H_2O, the
English language happens to have separate lexical items for its
three states of penetrability, namely *steam, water,* and *ice.* However, the specification [2 Penetrable] is in a sense unmarked,
since *ice* and *steam* are understood to be different states of
water, but we do not normally think of *steam,* for example, as
being a state of *ice.* For other objects, this abundance of lexical items does not exist, and an unmarked state of penetrability

is associated with each one. Thus *air, vapor, oxygen* are considered [1 Penetrable] unless otherwise specified; *milk, juice, coffee, blood, mercury* are [2 Penetrable]; and *glass, skin, wood, meat,* and *copper* are [3 Penetrable].

Another feature having a multiplicity of values, presumably, is Color; there does not seem to be a set of binary semantic features which organize our classification of the color adjectives *red, orange, yellow, green, blue, violet, brown,* and the like. Thus, we do not ordinarily think of any one color adjective as the antonym of any other, whereas we do have antonyms of adjectives which contain one or more binary features in their semantic representation, for example *tall* versus *short, loose* versus *tight,* and even *black* versus *white.*

The semantic representation of lexical items, however, cannot be effectively studied by examining words only in isolation; they must be studied also in terms of the relationships they enter into in sentences. Furthermore, the study of the semantic properties of constituents larger in size than lexical items deserves attention. We begin by inquiring what it is that accounts for our intuitions that certain sentences of English are internally contradictory while others are not.

Consider first of all the internally contradictory sentence 2.7, which we repeat here as 4.4 for convenience:

4.4   Harry drank a piece of paper.

as against the undisputedly non-odd sentence:

4.5   Harry drank a glass of water.

Informally, in Chapter 2, we described the contradiction in sentence 4.4 as arising from the fact that the verb *drink* requires that its object designate a liquid, but that the NP *a piece of paper* does not designate a liquid. Let us see if we can arrive at a more precise formulation of this description. On the basis of our earlier considerations, the lexical element *paper* may be said to have the semantic feature [3 Penetrable]. This specification, moreover, is a property of the NP *a piece of paper* as a whole.[10] We can now state the observation that the verb *drink* occurs only with [2 Penetrable] object noun phrases as a semantic feature of the verb which makes reference to the specification [2 Penetrable]. That feature may be written [___[2 Penetrable]], which we interpret as follows: the noun phrase following the verb *drink* is assigned the specification [2 Penetrable]. If that noun phrase already has the specification [2 Penetrable], for

---

[10] We refrain for the moment from formulating precisely how it is that an NP receives the semantic specifications belonging to the nouns it contains. This is an instance, the reader will recall, of the general process termed PROJECTION by Katz and Fodor (1963). This matter is taken up below.

example a glass of water, then no contradiction ensues, but if it has the specification [3 Penetrable], the contradiction is immediate. Suppose, however, the object NP is unspecified for Penetrable, as in the sentence:

4.6   Harry drank a lot of foul-smelling stuff.

In such cases, the specification [2 Penetrable] is simply imposed on the object noun phrase. Finally, suppose the feature Penetrable is inappropriate for the object noun phrase, as in the sentence:

4.7   Harry drank mysteries and detective stories.

Once again we can say that a contradiction arises, but it is one which is different in character from that of sentence 4.4. We are likely to view sentence 4.7 as a (not particularly striking) metaphor, but not sentence 4.4.

Following Chomsky (1965, Chapter 2), we call semantic features of verbs which make reference to semantic-feature specifications of noun phrases with which they occur SELECTIONAL FEATURES.[11] Selectional features for verbs are set up, not just on the basis of the specifications of their object noun phrases, but also on the basis of the specifications of their subject noun phrases. Thus *drink* also has the selectional feature [[+Animate]___] to indicate that the specification [+Animate] is associated with its subject noun phrase. Accordingly, we understand that sentence 4.5 is not contradictory, but that the following sentence is:

4.8   The table drank a glass of water.

because the NP *the table* has the feature [−Animate]. In a similar manner, selectional features can be established for every verb and adjective in the lexicon, and as we shall indicate presently, also for every noun.

The distinction between transitive and intransitive verbs can also be expressed in terms of features. We noted in Chapter 3 that verbs such as *take place, vanish,* and *go by* do not occur in *E*-grammatical sentences together with object NP's, and conversely *know* and *prefer* do. These observations can be represented by associating with the latter pair of verbs the feature [___NP], and with the former trio of verbs the feature [___]. Verbs having the feature [___NP] are those verbs which like

---

[11] The present account of selectional features differs in at least two respects from Chomsky's. First, Chomsky considers selectional features to be binary. Where we have simply [[+Animate]___], Chomsky has [+[+Animate]___] and [−[−Animate]___], which are interpreted to mean that the verb having these feature specifications appears only after [+Animate] subjects in fully grammatical sentences. Second, Chomsky's selectional features do not impose any specifications on subject and object noun phrases in case those noun phrases are in fact unspecified for the features referred to by the selectional features.

know and *prefer* are permitted to occur together with object NP's; verbs having the feature [___] are permitted to occur without such objects. On the basis of the grammaticality of such sentences as:

4.9 The Shadow knows.

we may assume that *know* has both the features [___NP] and [___].

These features, however, are not semantic ones such as the ones we have been considering up to this point in the present chapter. Unlike selectional features, they do not make reference to feature specifications of noun phrases, but merely to the presence or absence of noun phrases. They do not impose any features on noun phrases, and hence violation of them does not lead to internal contradiction; it leads to ungrammaticality. The term applied by Chomsky (1965, Chapter 2) to such features is STRICT SUBCATEGORIZATIONAL, since they can be thought of as subcategorizing verbs in accordance with their occurrence with other constituents which are themselves grammatical categories.[12]

The skepticism that we raised in the preceding chapter regarding the deep-structure validity of the notions subject and object obviously must be taken into consideration in any attempt to establish what are the selectional and strict subcategorizational features of verbs in English. Consider for example the problem of determining what these features are for the verbs *shake* and *dissolve,* which were used in our discussion in Chapter 3. For *shake,* we would be required to establish two lexical items, one with the strict subcategorizational feature [___] and the selectional feature [[−Abstract]___], and the other with the strict subcategorizational feature [___NP] and the selectional features [[+Animate]___] and [___[−Abstract]].[13] For *dissolve,* similarly, we would be required to distinguish at least two lexical items, one with the features [___] and [[3 Penetrable]___],

---

[12] Again, our account of strict subcategorizational features differs from that of Chomsky, who considers them also to be binary. According to his account, a verb such as *vanish* would receive both the specifications [+___] and [−___NP].

[13] This is actually far from an adequate representation of the selectional properties of *shake.* The subject of the transitive verb *shake* may not only be an animate NP, but also any NP designating force or something with force to it. Consider, for example, such sentences as:

    (i)   The wind shook the trees.
    (ii) The force of the blow shook the ground.

The object of *shake* may also have as its head one of a class of abstract N's such as *faith, trust, belief,* and the like as in the sentence:

    (iii) John's recent dealings have shaken my faith in his integrity.

Notice, too, that the subjects of such sentences designate such abstractions as events or ideas.

and the other with the features [___NP], [[2 Penetrable]___] and [___[3 Penetrable]]. But even with these features we have no means of talking about the instrumental or locative sense of the subject of such sentences as 3.23, the use of *dissolve* in sentence 3.24, or of the possibility that *dissolve* can occur with a [+Animate] subject, as in sentence 3.25. As we indicated in Chapter 3, we shall attempt a solution to the deep-structure subject-object problem in Chapter 6. For the time being we retain the position that there are subjects and objects in deep structure.

Before taking up the topic of how features are projected from lexical items to the constituents containing them, we need to make one more point concerning the semantic character of verbs and adjectives, namely that their entire semantic content is expressible in terms of selectional features. Another way of stating this is to say that the meaning of verbs and adjectives is totally involved in their relationships with NP's; in particular their meaning has to do with features which they impose on those NP's. We illustrate this point with a few examples. Consider first the sentence:

4.10   The boy is chasing a ball down the street.

In this example, the verb *chase* imposes on its [+Animate] subject a feature which indicates that it is in motion, and that it is moving intentionally; it imposes on its [−Abstract] object that it is also in motion and that it is moving away from the subject; it also imposes on both noun phrases that they are in the location designated by the prepositional phrase. That this is the case can be seen from considering a multiply contradictory sentence such as:

4.11   The boy standing on the step is chasing a ball which is rolling toward him through the front lawn down the street.

The sentence is internally contradictory since the subject of *chase* receives by projection features indicating that it is not in motion and not on the street, and the object of *chase* is similarly marked as moving toward the subject and being somewhere other than on the street.

Now consider the sentences:

4.12   The bartender made the martini.
4.13   The bartender drank the martini.

In 4.12, the verb *make* imposes on its object a feature which indicates that it has come into existence, while in 4.13, the verb *drink* imposes a feature on its object which is interpreted to mean that as such it no longer exists. Thus the sentence formed by conjoining sentences 4.12 and 4.13 in that order with the expression *and then* is not contradictory:

> **4.14** The bartender made the martini, and then he drank it.

whereas conjoining them in the other order leads to an internal contradiction:

> **4.15** The bartender drank the martini, and then he made it.

Finally, consider the following collection of examples:

> **4.16** That man is tall.
> **4.17** That baby is long.
> **4.18** That pole is tall.
> **4.19** That pole is long.
> **4.20** That building is tall.
> **4.21** That building is long.
> **4.22** That plot of land is deep.
> **4.23** That lake is deep.
> **4.24** That puddle is deep.
> **4.25** That man is well.
> **4.26** That woman is beautiful.

It is possible to draw a number of interesting observations about the features imposed on the subject noun phrases by the various adjectives *tall*, *long*, *deep*, *well*, and *beautiful* in these examples. The first three are all adjectives which measure space along particular dimensions. The use of *tall* imposes on its subject that it is being measured along the vertical dimension of ordinary perceptual space, where by vertical is meant perpendicular to the surface of the earth, while the use of *long* measures any single dimension which is not necessarily vertical. Examples 4.16 and 4.17 show us that the head-to-foot measurement of babies is not along the vertical axis, whereas that of men is. More precisely, we should say that if a sentence such as:

> **4.27** That baby is tall.

does not involve a contradiction, then we are prepared to perceive the subject NP *that baby* as referring to an upright object, but otherwise not. Similarly, from 4.18 and 4.19, we see that the use of the adjective *tall* imposes on the subject NP *that pole* that the REFERENT is vertical; the use of *long* does not impose any particular orientation feature on it. In 4.20 and 4.21, we have a subject NP *that building* whose inherent specifications indicate that it has both a vertical and an orthogonal nonvertical dimension, so that the adjective *tall* imposes no orientation on that NP, but simply a measure of its vertical dimension, while *long* is a measure of its other dimension. Finally, *deep* is a measure of two quite distinctly different dimensions. On the one hand, it is a measure of one dimension of two-dimensional objects not having any vertical dimension, and on the other it is a measure of that dimension (of three-dimensional objects having a surface) which is perpendicular to the surface. The interpretation imposed on particular subject noun phrases, of course, depends upon what the subject is. In 4.22 only the first interpretation is noncontradictory since the NP *that plot of land* is understood to be a non-vertical two-dimensional object, while in 4.23 and 4.24, the second sense is noncontradictory, since the noun phrases *that lake* and *that puddle* designate three-dimensional objects with surfaces.

Each of the adjectives *tall*, *long*, and *deep* has an antonymous counterpart in English; they are *short*, *short*, and *shallow*, respectively. The fact that *tall* and *long* have the same antonym indicates that the semantic distinction between them is neutralized when that antonym is used. More interesting is the fact that associated with each NP with which such adjectives are appropriately used is a standard of measurement by which the referents of such NP's are judged *tall* or *short*, *long* or *short*, *deep* or *shallow*. Thus, Lake Erie (*qua* lake or perhaps Great Lake) is *shallow*, even though its average depth is hundreds of feet, while a foot-deep puddle would certainly be judged *deep*. A man is judged *tall* if he exceeds a particular height, say six feet or so, while a three-foot-tall two-year-old child would be *tall*, too. In general, for these antonymous pairs, the point at which one switches from one to the other comes somewhere in the middle of some range of values appropriate to each NP.

The same, however, is not true for the antonymous pair *well* and *ill*. The adjective *well* measures a standard of health such that any deviation from it renders its subject *ill*. The cutoff point between *well* and *ill* then lies very close to an extreme end of the range of values covered by these terms. The following sentences have the same meaning:

> **4.28**   That man is not well.
> **4.29**   That man is ill.

But these do not:

> **4.30**   That man is not tall.
> **4.31**   That man is short.

There is a narrow indeterminate range of values between those that are clearly *tall* and those that are clearly *short*. Finally, the antonyms *moderate* and *extreme* present another, still different situation; *moderate* is appropriate only for qualities in the middle of the range indicated by these terms, while *extreme* denotes qualities at either end of the range. Consider the sentences:

>**4.32**   The political ideas of the candidate are not extreme.
>**4.33**   The political ideas of the candidate are not moderate.

From sentence 4.32, we may conclude that the candidate's political ideas are moderate, but from 4.33 we cannot conclude whether his views are extremely to the right or to the left.

The examples and discussion in this chapter should provide the reader with some feeling, at least, for the way in which verbs and adjectives impose feature specifications of various sorts upon NP's. We are now in a position to provide an account of how, within sentences, features associated with lexical items are projected onto the constituents containing them. First let us consider the way in which features of nouns are projected onto NP's. In case an NP consists solely of an N, the answer is obvious: all the semantic features of the N are simply projected onto the NP. In case an NP consists of an N and a relative clause, then all the semantic features of the N together with all the features imposed on that N by the verb or adjective in the relative clause are projected onto the NP. In case an NP consists of an N and another NP, then once again simply the semantic features of the N are projected onto the first NP. The subordinate NP has no effect on the semantic interpretation of the main N, but rather the main N imposes its features on the N in the subordinate NP in exactly the same way that a V imposes its features on the NP which are its subjects and objects. Thus, in the sentence:

>**4.34**   Peter lopped off the ear of the servant.

the NP *the ear of the servant* receives no feature specifications from the NP *the servant*, but of course it does from the verb *lop off*. Presumably also we would want to say that the NP *the servant* also receives these features, by virtue of the relationship between the servant and his ears, since it would be contradictory to add:

>**4.35**   But the servant was not thereby injured.

In case the NP consists of a conjunction of noun phrases, then the main NP receives all the features of the conjoined noun phrases which compose it. It must be pointed out, however, that these features are not simply scrambled up together; a conjoined NP such as *my mother and my father* does not simply have the specifications [−Masculine] and [+Masculine] (which would be contradictory). Rather it must be assumed that these specifications are somehow kept separate. One way to accomplish this is to assume that each noun in the lexicon has associated with it a REFERENTIAL INDEX, which is not generally fixed in advance, but which is free to take on the values 1, 2, 3, and so on. We may assume that in any discourse the first noun used is assigned the index 1, the next noun which refers to a different entity the index 2, and so on. Each time reference is made to something not previously referred to, the noun is assigned a new index number. Two nouns with the same referential index are said to be COREFERENTIAL. Noun phrases receive by projection the referential index of their head noun; in examples we shall indicate the referential index as a subscript. Note that two noun phrases can have the same referential index, yet be different in form; conversely noncoreferential occurrences of otherwise identical noun phrases can appear in the same sentence. For example:

4.36 Senator Dirksen$_1$ was in New York$_2$ yesterday; the Illinois Republican$_1$ appeared to be healthy.

4.37 The man$_1$ said that the man$_2$ was coming.

4.38 The man$_1$ said that he$_1$ was coming.

From example 4.38, we see also that pronominalization depends upon coreferentiality. This matter is taken up in Chapter 5, section 5.

Returning now to the problem of the projected features of an NP made up of conjoined noun phrases, we find that such an NP receives as its referential index the conjunction of the indices of the noun phrases which it comprises, and the specifications it receives from its conjuncts may be considered to have the indices of the NP's supplying them.[14] Thus the NP *my mother$_1$ and my father$_2$* has the referential indices 1 and 2 and the features, among others, [−Masculine]$_1$ and [+Masculine]$_2$. This is true, furthermore, whether the compound NP arises from rule 3.58(i) or from the application of conjunction reduction to conjoined sentences. Notice now that plural noun phrases, for example, *my parents*, can be considered to arise from the conjunction of singular noun phrases which are identical in every respect except for their referential indices. In the case of *my parents* we know that exactly two noun phrases have been conjoined: *my parent$_1$ and my parent$_2$*. In the case of an NP such as *my friends*, on the other hand, an unspecified number of singular noun phrases having different referential indices have been conjoined.

Finally, in case the NP consists of an S, the NP receives by projection the specifications of that S. So far, we have not said anything about the semantic representation of sentences. As we

---

[14] Also in the case of an NP not made up of conjoined NP's, we may assume that its referential index is that of its head noun.

shall see, it is not at all easy to deal with the semantic properties of sentences. If we restrict our attention just to sentences
which occur as noun phrases, we find that their semantic representation can be thought of as being made up of the specifications of their subject and object noun phrases and of certain
constant specifications. These constant specifications are [+Ab-
stract] and a referential index. The fact that sentences which
function as noun phrases are [+Abstract] means that their occurrence as subject or object of verbs which impose the specification [−Abstract] on them results in a contradiction, as in
sentences 3.11 and 3.12. The fact that they have a referential
index of their own means that they are always singular, and
that if repeated in a discourse, the second occurrence may be
replaced by a pronoun, as in:

> **4.39**   The professor had forgotten that classes had
> been called off, but later he remembered it.

The specifications of the subject and object noun phrases of
a sentence can be thought of as what the sentence is about, and
hence clearly they must form a part of the semantic representations of the sentence as a whole. Thus when a sentence functions
as, say, the object of a verb such as *confess*, the verb may impose specifications on the sentence, which are specifications of
the subject and object of the sentence. Consider, for example:

> **4.40**   I confessed that I had committed the crime.
> **4.41**   I confessed that you had committed the crime.
> **4.42**   I confessed that I had done nothing wrong.
> **4.43**   I confessed that I had committed suicide.

Among the specifications imposed by the verb *confess* on its object sentence are (1) the subject of *confess* and the subject of
the object sentence must be coreferential, (2) the subject of the
object sentence must be [+Living], and (3) the object of the object sentence must be a social wrong. Consequently, sentence
4.40 is noncontradictory, whereas 4.41–4.43 are all contradictory
because of a violation of some one of the three impositions just
mentioned.[15]

This all but completes our account of the way in which noun

---

[15] This account of the properties of *confess* is overly simple. Example 4.41, is not contradictory if, for example, you and I are accomplices in the crime. This can be seen by considering
the sentence:

  (i)   I confessed that you had committed the crime while I was out front looking for the
     cops.

Another case in which the subject of the subordinate clause does not have to be coreferential with the subject of *confess* is when some other NP in the subordinate clause is coreferential with it, as in:

phrases receive their semantic interpretations. We have in principle, at least, given a full account also of how sentences receive
their semantic specifications, since, as we have observed, verbs
contribute no independent meaning to a sentence but only impose components of meaning on noun phrases. Of course, to com-
lete this picture of how sentences are meaningful, we shall
also have to say in some detail how adverbial expressions and
such elements as the tense of the verb and negation contribute
to the meaning of sentences. But before this can be done, much
more about the syntactic properties of these things has to be
discussed; this is done in Chapter 6. Moreover, we shall have to
give an account of such sentence forms as questions and commands, whose meanings obviously differ significantly from the
meanings of ordinary propositions. This is also done in Chapter
6. The one remaining point to be made in this chapter is that the
semantic features of nouns must also be regarded as selectional
features.

We have already observed that nouns having the strict subcategorizational feature [___NP] impose feature specifications
on the noun phrase following them; for example, the noun *paw*
has the selectional feature [___[+Animate]]. But practially
all nouns, regardless of their strict subcategorizational features, can occur in sentences as so-called predicate nouns, in
which case they impose on their subjects exactly those feature
specifications we have hitherto considered to be a part of their
semantic representations. Consider, for example, the following
sentences:

4.44 That woman is the wife of the mayor.
4.45 That person is the wife of the mayor.
4.46 That man is the wife of the mayor.

In order to account for the contradictory character of 4.46, and
for the fact that in 4.45 the specification [−Masculine] is imposed
on the subject NP *that person*, we must assume that the predicate NP *the wife of the mayor*, and hence the N *wife*, have the

---

(ii) I confessed to my history professor that his discussion of the wars of succession
made no sense to me at all.

Finally, notice that the following sentences are exactly parallel to 4.40-4.43 with regard to their status as contradictory or noncontradictory:

(iii) I confessed my sin.
(iv) I confessed your sin.
(v) I confessed my act of heroism.
(vi) I confessed my suicide.

Among other things this suggests that the *my* in example (i) stands in exactly the same
relation to the N *sin* as *I* does to the VP *had committed the crime* in example 4.40. This
observation, incidentally, supports our contention in Chapter 3 that the subject-object
framework is inadequate for the syntactic description of English.

selectional feature [[−Masculine]___]. A moment's reflection should convince the reader that all nouns have selectional features which exactly match their semantic-feature specifications. As another example, consider the subclass of nouns which are known as collective nouns; such nouns, for example, *family, group, committee, herd*, are said to refer to collections of things having certain properties. But consider such sentences as these (the second of which is contradictory):

> **4.47** The Richardsons are a happy family.
> **4.48** Richardson is a happy family.

These sentences make clear that such nouns must be considered to have a selectional feature which indicates that their subject has a conjunction of referential indices; in the case of *family*, each of these is associated with an NP with the specification [+Human].[16]

Thus, semantically, nouns and verbs differ only slightly, the only difference being that if a noun has a feature [[+F]___], where F is some feature, then it also has the specification [+F]. In Chapter 5, we shall see how even this difference can be eliminated.

---

[16] Like other kinship terms, however, *family* may be used to designate not only particular groups of humans, but also such things as animals, nations, and languages. Thus we speak of the Indo-European family of languages, of Greek and Latin as daughters of Proto-Indo-European (which is the parent language), and of English and German as sister languages (having sprung from a common parent). The full range of kinship system is, of course, not used — we do not need to make gender distinctions, for example (but it is interesting to note that the female terms are generally employed wherever there is a choice) — although if we wanted to we could make use of many which are not customarily employed. For example, we could call ancient Greek an aunt of French, and designate Spanish and English as cousin languages.

5 SOME TRANSFORMATIONS IN ENGLISH

In this chapter we shall consider in some detail the nature of a few of those rules which convert deep structures of sentences of English into their surface-structure forms. We begin by considering some of the examples we have already presented in Chapters 2-4, which we said had the property that their deep and surface structures do not match.

TRANSFORMATIONS RELATING TO EXTRAPOSITION

Consider first of all examples 3.13 and 3.14, repeated here for convenience:

>**5.1 (= 3.13)** That the president of the ladies' auxiliary is really bald comes as no surprise to many people.
>**5.2 (= 3.14)** It comes as no surprise to many people that the president of the ladies' auxiliary is really bald.

In Chapter 3 we pointed out that the deep-structure subject of 5.2 has been shifted to the end of the sentence, leaving behind the pronoun *it* in the position formerly occupied by the deep-structure subject of sentence 5.2 as in Fig. 5.1. We have used triangles to stand for the internal structure of the sentence that is irrelevant to the present discussion. Upon application of the rule which shifts the subject clause to the end of the sentence, the structure which results is that shown in Fig. 5.2. As indicated in Chapter 3, the name given to this rule is extraposition.

The rule of extraposition can be thought of as applying in two steps. The first step copies the subject clause at the end of

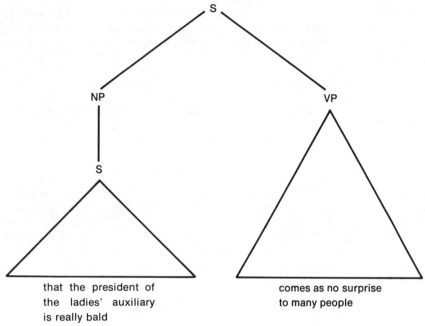

that the president of
the ladies' auxiliary
is really bald

comes as no surprise
to many people

Fig. 5.1. Deep structure of sentence 5.2.

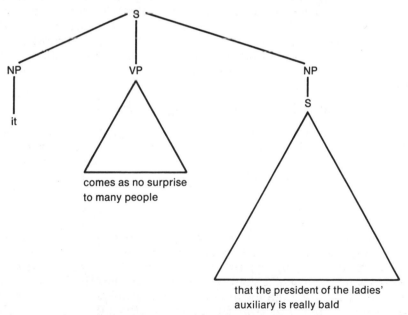

it

comes as no surprise
to many people

that the president of the ladies'
auxiliary is really bald

Fig. 5.2. Surface structure of sentence 5.2

the sentence containing it, and the second step replaces the original occurrence of the subject clause by the pronoun *it*. Other sentences in which the rule of extraposition has applied are the following:

5.3 It pleases me that everyone has managed to figure out what I was trying to say.
5.4 It is said that few people return from that place alive.
5.5 It seems that the wind has shifted direction in the last half hour.
5.6 I take it that you plan to resign.

In sentence 5.3, the subject clause *that everyone ... trying to say* has been moved to the end of the sentence; similarly in sentence 5.4, the subject clause *that few people ... alive* has been moved to the end of the sentence. In sentence 5.5, however, not only has the subject clause *that the wind ... last half hour* been so moved, the linguistic object in which that clause has not been moved is *E*-ungrammatical:

5.7 *That the wind has shifted direction in the last half hour seems.

The difference between sentence 5.5 and 5.2–5.4 is that the rule of extraposition must be applied to the deep structure underlying 5.5, but not to those underlying 5.2–5.4. Finally, in sentence 5.6, the object clause *that you ... resign* has been extraposed, leaving behind the pronoun *it* in the position of the original direct object. As in the case of 5.5, extraposition must be applied to the deep structure underlying sentence 5.6, since the following is also *E*-ungrammatical:

5.8 *I take that you plan to resign.

We say that the application of the rule of extraposition to the deep structures underlying sentences 5.2–5.4 is OPTIONAL, whereas its application to those underlying sentences 5.5–5.6 is OBLIGATORY.

Now consider the following sentence, a paraphrase of sentence 3.1:

5.9 Politicians know that voters prefer results.

Since the pronoun *it* does not appear in this sentence, it would seem that the rule of extraposition has not applied to the deep structure underlying it; in other words that extraposition is INAPPLICABLE to such a deep structure. Alternatively, we could maintain that the application of extraposition to this deep structure is obligatory, but that the pronoun *it* is subsequently obligatorily deleted following a verb such as *know*. What evidence is there that would support one or the other of these positions?

One piece of evidence that supports the second position is that adverbial expressions, such as *well*, may occur in sentences like 5.9 between the verb and the object clause, but not following the object clause as a whole. Thus we have:

> **5.10** Politicians know well that voters prefer results.

but not:

> **5.11** *Politicians know that voters prefer results well.

On the other hand, such expressions do not generally intervene between the verb and an object NP which is not a clause.[1] We have:

> **5.12** Politicians know campaign trips well.

but not:

> **5.13** *Politicians know well campaign trips.

The reason that this evidence supports the second position is that this position explains why it is that clausal but not other direct objects follow adverbial modifiers of the verb *know*. Presumably in the deep structures underlying both sentences 5.10 and 5.12, the adverbial modifier follows the direct object, but extraposition applies to the structure underlying 5.10 to copy the object clause on the other side of the adverbial modifier. A subsequent transformational rule would then be required to delete the pronoun *it* standing for the original object clause. This rule, which we may call simply *it*-deletion, applies obligatorily when the pronoun follows such verbs as *know, understand, expect*, and so forth, but is inapplicable when it follows a verb such as *take, hate*, and the like.[2]

From these two examples of transformational rules in English, extraposition and *it*-deletion, we can extract four general principles concerning such rules. The first is that for a transformation to apply to a particular deep structure it must contain particular constituents in particular relations to the rest of the deep structure. The rule of extraposition thus applies only to

---

[1] When, however, the object NP contains a clause modifying the head noun, then the adverb may directly follow the verb or it may even be placed between the head noun and the clause. Consider for example such sentences as:

    (i)   I know well the songs that were popular ten years ago.
   (ii)   I know the songs that were popular ten years ago well.
  (iii)   I know the songs well that were popular ten years ago.

[2] Thus, example 5.8 is ungrammatical not only because extraposition must apply to object clauses following *take*, but also because *it*-deletion is inapplicable when that pronoun follows *take*.

deep structures containing clauses occurring as subject or object, not to deep structures not containing such clauses. Deep structures to which such a rule is applicable are said to SATISFY the structural requirements of that rule.

Second, whether a transformational rule applies obligatorily or optionally to a particular deep structure which satisfies it is a consequence of some further condition holding in that structure. Extraposition, for example, obligatorily applies in case the clause which is to be copied at the end of a sentence is either an object clause or the subject clause of an intransitive verb, such as *seem*.[3] It applies optionally in case the clause to be copied is the subject of a transitive verb such as *please;* of an adjective such as *probable*, or of a passive verb such as *said*.

Third, whether a structure even satisfies the requirements of a transformation may depend on the choice of particular lexical items in that structure. We have seen, for example, that the applicability of *it*-deletion following verbs depends on the choice of the verb. Fourth and finally, the application of transformations is sequentially ordered. For example, the rule of extraposition must be applied before the rule of *it*-deletion, since the latter rule would have no structures to apply to if extraposition were not applied first.

The conditions under which the clause-introducer *that* may be deleted illustrates several of these points. It was noted in Chapter 3 that this word may not be deleted if it introduces a nonextraposed subject clause; otherwise it may optionally be deleted. We may say that this rule is satisfied by any structure containing an extraposed clause, the effect of the rule being the deletion of the clause-introducer *that*. Clearly, then, this rule, like the *it*-deletion rule, requires the prior application of the extraposition transformation. The rule, moreover, is virtually always optional; there are almost no additional conditions under which it is obligatory or inapplicable.[4]

THE INFINITIVAL CLAUSE SEPARATION TRANSFORMATION

Related to the rule of extraposition is a transformational rule that has an effect on deep-structure subject or object clauses

---

[3] Examples such as:

> That John was right all along seems clear.

are not counterexamples to this claim, since the deep structure subject of *seems* is not *that John was right all along* but rather *that John was right all along to be clear*. The *that*-clause is then made subject of *seems* by the rule considered in the next section, namely the infinitive-clause separation transformation. For further discussion, see pp. 65–66.

[4] We shall see when we discuss the various transformations having to do with relative clause formation that there is one condition under which *that*-deletion is obligatory.

which, instead of being introduced by *that*, contain the so-called
INFINITIVE form of the verb. The infinitive verb form in English
is generally indicated by the presence of an immediately preceding *to;* clauses containing such verb forms are known as infinitival clauses. Consider first of all example 2.38, which is repeated here as 5.14:

> **5.14 (= 2.38)** I began to wonder whether anyone was
> interested in me.

Suppose we take the deep structure of 5.14 to be that represented
in Fig. 5.3. To obtain the surface structure of this sentence,

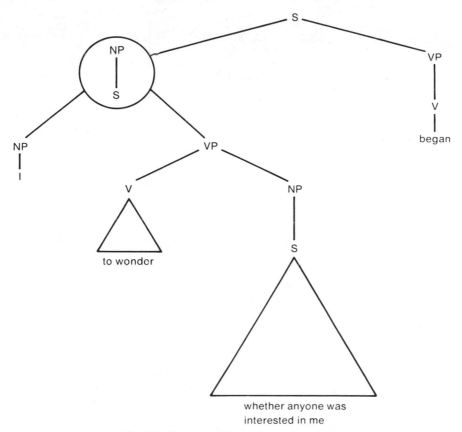

Fig. 5.3. Deep structure of sentence 5.14.

which is indicated in Fig. 5.4, a transformation must be applied
to move the predicate of the infinitival clause so that it becomes
a constituent of the predicate of sentence 5.14. The subject of
the infinitival clause, by this rule, then becomes the surface-
structure subject of sentence 5.14. Like the rule of extraposition,

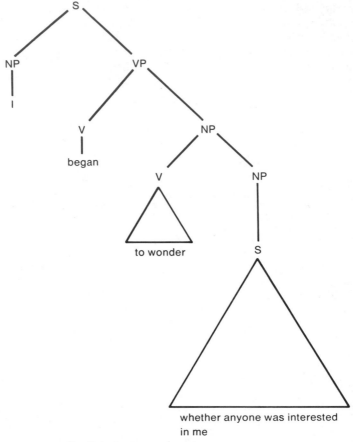

Fig. 5.4. Surface structure of sentence 5.14.

this rule can be thought of as proceeding in two steps. The first step copies the predicate of the infinitival clause as a constituent of the predicate of the entire sentence. The second step simply deletes the predicate of the infinitival clause in its original position, together with the constituents NP and S corresponding to those circled in Fig. 5.3, since these constituents play no role in the surface structure of sentences like 5.14. We may call this rule the infinitival clause separation transformation.

The same rule applies to the deep structure of example 2.39, which is repeated here as 5.15:

5.15 (= 2.39)　The general expects the enemy machine-gun nest to be wiped out by nightfall.

The deep structure of sentence 5.15 is represented in Fig. 5.5. The surface structure of that sentence, which is obtained by

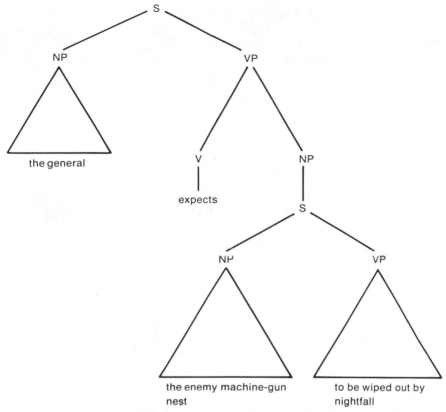

Fig. 5.5. Deep structure of sentence 5.15.

application of the infinitival clause separation transformation, is given in Fig. 5.6. The application of the infinitival clause separation transformation to object infinitival clauses results in no change in the order of constituents, only in their structural relationships to one another. Later on in this chapter, evidence will be presented that such an alteration in the structural relationships in sentences such as 5.15 does indeed take place; such evidence cannot be presented at this point in the discussion simply because other material must first be presented for the argument to be convincing.

The difference between the effects of the extraposition transformation and those of the infinitival separation transformation can best be seen by examining their application to two deep structures which are identical except that one has a *that*-clause and the other an infinitival clause. Two such deep structures are given in Figs. 5.7 and 5.8. Upon applying the extraposition transformation to the deep structure of 5.7 and the infinitival

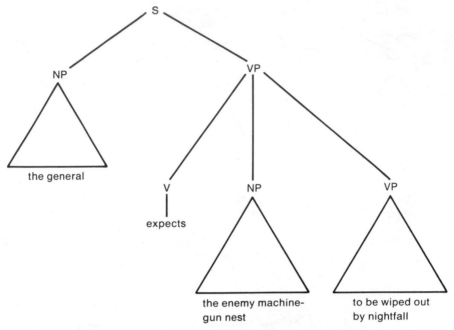

Fig. 5.6. Surface structure of sentence 5.15, obtained from the deep structure of that sentence by application of the infinitival clause separation transformation.

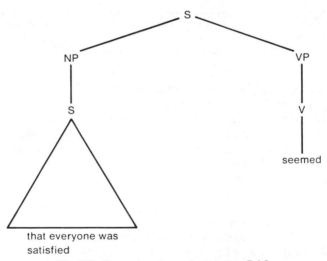

Fig. 5.7. Deep structure of sentence 5.16.

clause separation transformation to the deep structure of 5.8, we obtain the surface structures given in Figs. 5.9 and 5.10. They are sentences 5.16 and 5.17.

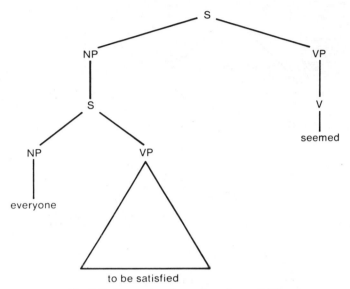

Fig. 5.8. Deep structure of sentence 5.17.

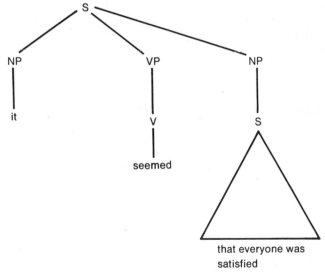

Fig. 5.9. Surface structure of sentence 5.16.

5.16 It seemed that everyone was satisfied.
5.17 Everyone seemed to be satisfied.

Despite the gross difference between the surface structures of sentences 5.16 and 5.17, these two sentences are practically, if

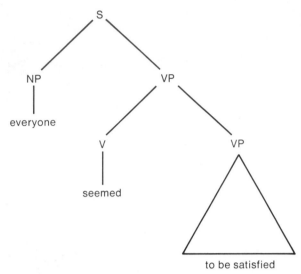

Fig. 5.10. Surface structure of sentence 5.17.

not totally, identical in meaning. We have accounted for this fact by providing these sentences with practically identical deep structures which undergo different transformational rules. Notice that the structure represented in Fig. 5.10 may undergo one more transformation, namely a rule which deletes *to be*, resulting in the sentence:

5.18 Everyone seemed satisfied.

The *to be*-deletion transformation applies optionally in this case; depending on the preceding verb, however, the rule may be either obligatory or inapplicable. It is inapplicable in case the preceding verb is, for example, *happen;* thus we have the sentence:

5.19 Everyone happened to be satisfied.

but not:

5.20 *Everyone happened satisfied.

It is obligatory in case the preceding verb is, for example, *feel;* thus we have:

5.21 Everyone felt satisfied.

but not:

5.22 *Everyone felt to be satisfied.

There are sentences in English having deep structures to which both the extraposition and infinitival-clause separation transformations apply. Consider for example sentence 5.23.

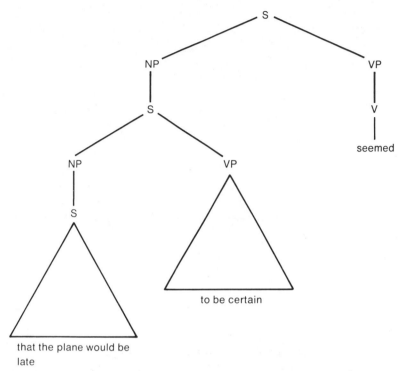

Fig. 5.11. Deep structure of sentence 5.23.

5.23 It seemed to be certain that the plane would be late.

This sentence has the deep structure shown in Fig. 5.11. To obtain the surface structure of sentence 5.23, which is represented in Fig. 5.12, the extraposition transformation must apply—to copy the *that*-clause at the end of the subordinate clause in which it occurs and to replace the original with the pronoun *it*. Then the infinitival-clause separation transformation must apply to convert *it* into the surface-structure subject of the entire sentence, and to copy the predicate of the infinitival clause together with the extraposed *that*-clause as constituents of the predicate of the entire sentence.

If we examine the deep structure pictured in Fig. 5.11, we find that the application of the extraposition transformation to it is optional. If this transformation is not applied, we obtain the following sentence:

5.24 That the plane would be late seemed to be certain.

with the surface structure shown in Fig. 5.13. Finally, it is possible to apply the *that*-deletion transformation and the *to be-*

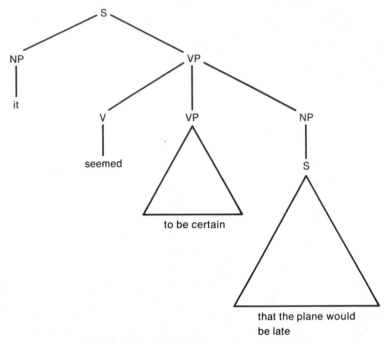

Fig. 5.12. Surface structure of sentence 5.23.

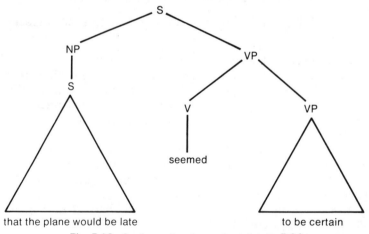

Fig. 5.13. Surface structure of sentence 5.24.

deletion transformation, with the consequence that all the following sentences can also be obtained in English:

5.25 It seemed certain that the plane would be late.
5.26 It seemed to be certain the plane would be late.
5.27 It seemed certain the plane would be late.
5.28 That the plane would be late seemed certain.

In Fig. 5.14 we indicate which transformations have been applied in order to obtain each of the sentences 5.23–5.28 from the deep structure represented in Fig. 5.11.

	Sentence					
Transformation	5.23	5.24	5.25	5.26	5.27	5.28
Extraposition	x		x	x	x	
Inf. clause sep.	x	x	x	x	x	x
That-deletion				x	x	
To-be-deletion			x		x	x

Fig. 5.14. Tabulation of transformations used to obtain sentences 5.23–5.28 from the deep structure represented in Fig. 5.11.

Similarly, it is possible for the same transformation—for example, extraposition or infinitival-clause separation—to apply more than once to a particular deep structure. Extraposition, for example, may apply twice to the deep structure given in Fig. 5.15, with the result that the surface structure given in Fig. 5.16 is obtained. The sentence which is obtained is of course:

5.29 It seemed that it was certain that the plane would be late.

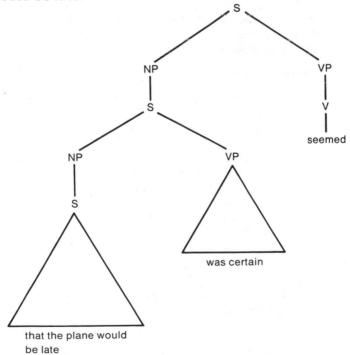

Fig. 5.15. Deep structure of sentence 5.29.

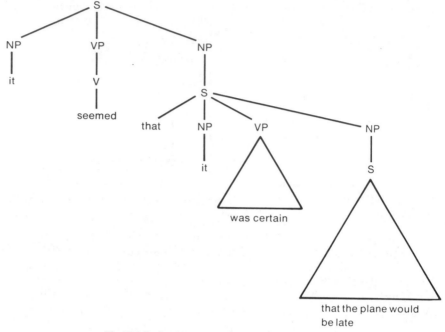

Fig. 5.16. Surface structure of sentence 5.29.

Infinitival clause separation, likewise, may apply twice to the deep structure represented in Fig. 5.17, resulting in the surface structure shown in Fig. 5.18. The sentence obtained is:

5.30 The plane seemed to be certain to be late.

Sentence 5.30, while certainly *E*-grammatical, is less acceptable stylistically than 5.31, in which *to be*-deletion has been applied:

5.31 The plane seemed certain to be late.

But that matter need not concern us here.[5]

Let us leave for the time being the extraposition and infinitival-clause separation transformations to consider other transformational rules in English; we shall return to consider these transformations in greater detail later in this chapter and again in Chapter 6. We now take up some transformations which are satisfied by deep structures containing nouns modified by relative clauses.

---

[5] The reason for the awkwardness of 5.30 probably has to do with the presence of a sequence of infinitives. Even sentences in which the sequence is unavoidable (because *to be*-deletion is inapplicable) are stylistically awkward, for example:

Everyone wants to be sure to be present at the inauguration.

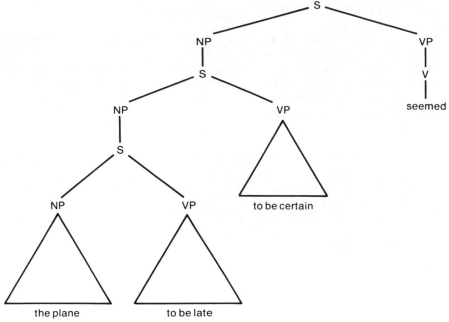

Fig. 5.17. Deep structure of sentence 5.30.

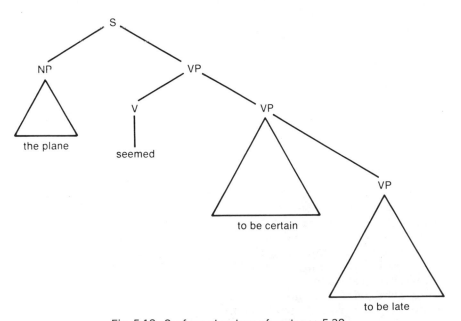

Fig. 5.18. Surface structure of sentence 5.30.

RELATIVE CLAUSE TRANSFORMATIONS

As we observed in Chapter 3, a transformational rule is required to replace with an appropriate relative pronoun an NP in a relative clause coreferential with the N modified by the relative clause. The rule also must have the effect of moving the pronoun to the beginning of the relative clause. We postulate for the following sentence:

5.32 The man who just left needs help.

the deep structure as indicated in Fig. 5.19 (ignoring for the present the deep-structure status of *the*). The transformational rule just mentioned must convert this structure into the surface structure given in Fig. 5.20.

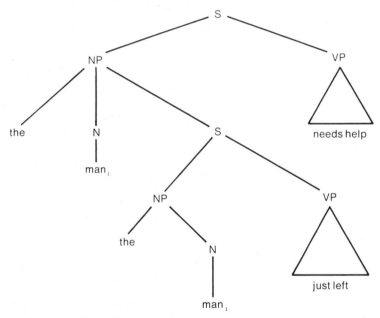

Fig. 5.19. Deep structure for sentence 5.32.

Again, as in the case of the extraposition and infinitival-clause separation transformations, we can think of the relative pronoun formation transformation as proceeding in two steps. First, the coreferential NP in the relative clause is moved to the front of the clause; and second, it is replaced by the appropriate relative pronoun. In case the NP has the specification [+Human], the relative pronoun is generally either *who, whom,* or *that;* otherwise it is generally either *which* or *that.* The relative pronoun *that* may be used regardless of what feature specifications the antecedent NP has.

In case the coreferential NP in the relative clause is not the

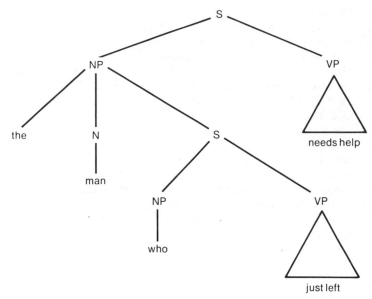

Fig. 5.20. Surface structure for sentence 5.32.

subject of that clause, it may optionally be deleted. Thus the following sentences all result from the same deep structure; the last of these is obtained by application of the relative pronoun deletion transformation:

5.33 Voters who(m) politicians know prefer results.
5.34 Voters that politicians know prefer results.
5.35 (= 3.9) Voters politicians know prefer results.

The relative pronoun deletion transformation is not satisfied by structures in which the relative pronoun stands for the subject of the relative clause; the following examples are both *E*-ungrammatical:

5.36 *The man just left needs help.
5.37 *Margie wears clothes are attractive to men.

But, as we indicated in Chapter 3, there is an optional transformation which does delete the relative pronoun standing for the subject of the relative clause, provided it is also followed by a form of the verb *be*, which the transformation also deletes. Thus the following sentences all result from the same deep structure:

5.38 (= 3.42) Margie wears clothes which are attractive to men.
5.39 Margie wears clothes that are attractive to men.
5.40 (= 3.43) Margie wears clothes attractive to men.

We may also note the transformation which applies if, upon application of the relative pronoun plus *be*-deletion rule, what is left after the noun is an expression ending in an adjective. This transformation copies the expression in front of the noun and deletes the expression after the noun. As we observed in Chapter 3, it is this transformation (which we may call the adjective preposing transformation) which enables us to say that sentences 3.44 and 3.45 arise from the same deep structure. We will have more to say about the adjective preposing transformation below.

In case the coreferential NP in the relative clause follows a preposition, the preposition may optionally be moved to the front of the relative clause, together with that NP. If so, however, the relative pronoun *that* may not be used and the form *whom* must be used; such constructions being characteristic of formal English. Thus all of the following sentences may be obtained from the same deep structure:

5.41 There is the person with whom I talked last night.

5.42 There is the person who(m) I talked with last night.

5.43 There is the person that I talked with last night.

5.44 There is the person I talked with last night.

Similarly, the following sentences arise from the same deep structure:

5.45 This is the bench under which the town drunk usually sleeps.

5.46 This is the bench which the town drunk usually sleeps under.

In the following special cases the relative pronouns which may be used are *when, where,* and *why,* respectively, the preposition being deleted: (1) the antecedent noun is one of time and the preposition is *at;* (2) the antecedent noun is one of place and the preposition is *in, at,* or *on;* and (3) the antecedent is the noun *reason* and the preposition is *for.* This observation accounts for the appearance of these relative pronouns in examples 3.37–3.39, and for the fact that the following sentences, along with 3.38 (which we repeat) are obtained from the same deep structure:

5.47 (= 3.38) This is the town where we were arrested last spring for parading without a permit.

5.48 This is the town in which we were arrested last spring for parading without a permit.

5.49 This is the town which we were arrested in last spring for parading without a permit.

5.50 This is the town that we were arrested in last spring for parading without a permit.

5.51 This is the town we were arrested in last spring for parading without a permit.

So far, in our consideration of relative-clause formation, the coreferential NP in the relative clause has not been a constituent of a subordinate sentence within that relative clause. However, it is possible for the coreferential NP to so occur, as in the following examples:

5.52 I don't think I'll be able to recognize the person who(m) they expect me to meet this afternoon at the airport.

5.53 I just spoke to the man who everyone hopes will oppose the mayor in the next election.

5.54 I just spoke to the man who(m) everyone hopes that the President will appoint to the vacant Cabinet post.

In sentence 5.52, the coreferential NP occurs as the direct object of the infinitive *to meet*, which is in turn the main verb of the clause, which is subordinate to the main verb of the relative clause, *expect*. Similarly, in 5.54 the coreferential NP occurs as the direct object of the main verb, *appoint*, of the subordinate clause, which is in turn the direct object of the main verb of the relative clause, *hopes*. In 5.53, on the other hand, it is the subject of the *that*-clause object of the verb of the relative clause; but notice that if the *that* is not deleted, the example is *E*-ungrammatical:

5.55 *I just spoke to the man who everyone hopes that will oppose the mayor in the next election.

This is the situation which was referred to in footnote 4; the subordinating conjunction *that* must be deleted when the subject of the clause has been removed, because it is the coreferential NP in a relative clause. For the present, we can give no explanation for this fact; we simply record it as an interesting though puzzling fact about English.[6] Another puzzling fact that we might also indicate here is that it is not possible to form an English sentence in which the coreferential NP is a constituent of a subject *that*-clause unless the clause is extraposed[7]:

5.56 *I just spoke to the man who/that will oppose the mayor in the next election annoys the party machine.

---

[6] For an attempt at an explanation, see Langendoen (forthcoming a).

[7] For an attempted explanation, see Ross (1967). Ross's work, incidentally, deals in an insightful fashion with a large number of very complex syntactic problems, some of which are only touched on or are completely ignored in this book.

5.57 I just spoke to the man who it annoys the party machine will oppose the mayor in the next election.

5.58 *I just spoke to the man who/that is clairvoyant is true.

5.59 I just spoke to the man who it is true is clairvoyant.

Now consider the following pairs of sentences:

5.60 The report that my neighbors were spreading about me was untrue.

5.61 The report that tuition was going up again in the fall was untrue.

In sentence 5.60, the clause *that ... about me*, which modifies the noun *rumor*, is clearly a relative clause; the relative pronoun *that* is understood to be the direct object of the verb *spread* in the relative clause. However, in sentence 5.61, the clause *that tuition ... the fall* is not a relative clause at all, since no NP which is coreferential to *report* is understood to occur in the deep structure underlying that clause. This distinction is reflected by the fact that in 5.60, *that* is a relative pronoun, while in 5.61 it is a subordinating conjunction. In 5.60, *that* may be replaced by *which*, with no loss of grammaticality, but not in 5.61. The question, then, is this: What is the deep-structure relationship between the noun *report* and the *that*-clause of sentence 5.61?

Two possibilities immediately suggest themselves. The first is that the relative pronoun plus *be*-deletion transformation has been applied to the structure underlying sentence 5.61, and that the deep structure of that sentence is as in Fig. 5.21. If the relative pronoun plus *be*-deletion transformation is not applied, however, then presumably the following would be obtained:

5.62 *The report which was that tuition was going up again in the fall was untrue.

Example 5.62 is *E*-ungrammatical. There is an *E*-grammatical sentence in English made up of the same words and in the same order; however, that sentence is written with the relative clause separated off by commas. The commas correspond to breaks in the INTONATION PATTERN of the sentence when it is spoken:

5.63 The report, which was that tuition was going up again in the fall, was untrue.

Such relative clauses arise from quite different deep structures than do the relative clauses we have been considering so far in this chapter (the distinction between the two kinds of relative clauses will be discussed further below), and this fact leads us to

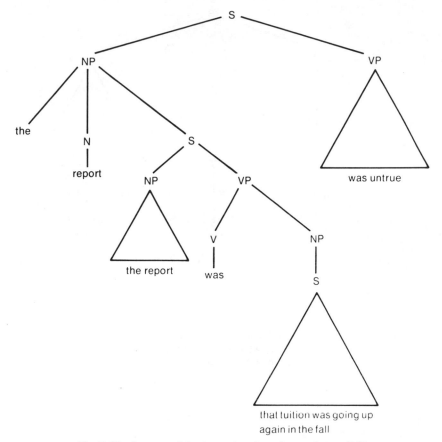

Fig. 5.21. One possible deep structure for sentence 5.61.

suspect that Fig. 5.21 does not provide the correct deep structure for sentence 5.61.

The second possibility is that sentence 5.61 has the deep structure roughly shown in Fig. 5.22. This deep structure is both syntactically and semantically motivated. Syntactically, the relationship between the N *report* and that *that*-clause in the deep structure of Fig. 5.22 is the same as that which we know to hold between the verb *report* and the *that*-clause in a sentence such as the following:

> **5.64** Some students reported that tuition was going up again in the fall.

This is a point in favor of the structure given in Fig. 5.22, since one would expect that nouns and verbs of directly related meaning and pronunciation would enter the same syntactic relation-

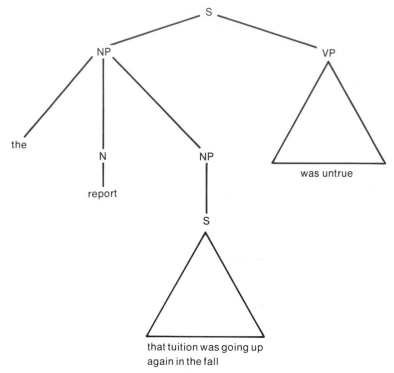

Fig. 5.22. Another possible deep structure for sentence 5.61.

ships. Semantically, the deep structure given in Fig. 5.22 is well motivated, since on the basis of it we would expect that the noun *report* imposes feature specifications on the *that*-clause, and not vice versa (compare our discussion in Chapter 4 concerning the imposition of features by head nouns of noun phrases on other noun phrases within those phrases). Clearly this is what happens; in sentence 5.61 the *that*-clause is understood as having been reported (and hence not necessarily true). On the other hand, from the deep structure given in Fig. 5.21, we would be led to expect the *that*-clause to impose specifications on *report*, since the clause occurs as the predicate of the N in the relative clause.

Both relative clauses and clauses such as the *that*-clause of 5.64 which function as NP objects of nouns may undergo extraposition. Thus, from the same deep structures that underlie sentences 5.60 and 5.61, we can obtain these sentences as well:

    5.65 The report was untrue that my neighbors were spreading about me.

    5.66 The report was untrue that tuition was going up again in the fall.

In light of these examples, the extraposition transformation which we discussed earlier should either be generalized so that the deep structures underlying sentences such as 5.65 and 5.66 satisfy it, or we should postulate another transformation which is satisfied only by deep structures such as these. As evidence for the latter position, consider the fact that the conditions under which extraposition of relative clauses or of NP objects of nouns is optional or inapplicable (it is never obligatory) differ from the conditions under which extraposition of clauses constituting entire NP's is obligatory or optional (it is never inapplicable). Extraposition of relative clauses or of NP objects of nouns is optional when they occur in NP's which are subjects of intransitive verbs. Thus we have:

> **5.67** Evidence that smoking is correlated with incidence of lung cancer was discussed.
> **5.68** Evidence was discussed that smoking is correlated with incidence of lung cancer.
> **5.69** The witness disappeared who held the key to the prosecution's case.
> **5.70** The witness who held the key to the prosecution's case disappeared.

Such extraposition is sometimes applicable when the verb is transitive. Thus we have:

> **5.71** The fact that no artifacts could be found there puzzled the archeologist.
> **5.72** The fact puzzled the archeologist that no artifacts could be found there.

Extraposition is apparently inapplicable, however, if the clause, if extraposed, could be mistaken for a modifier of the object NP. Thus we have:

> **5.73** The car which hit the lamp post also ran into the tree.
> **5.74** The car also ran into the tree which hit the lamp post.

But sentence 5.74 is not interpreted as containing an extraposed relative clause modifier of the subject; rather, the relative clause occurring in it is interpreted only as modifying the object NP.

Several other matters related to relative clause formation should also be considered. One is that, under certain conditions, the relative pronoun and its antecedent may be expressed in surface structure by the same word. The following examples are illustrative:

> **5.75** Moneylenders generally know who(m) they can trust to pay them back.

5.76 Fred often thinks about what no one else is thinking about at the time.

5.77 We live where there are no gas or sewer mains.

5.78 Stop whenever you feel tired.

5.79 I fail to understand how this device works.

5.80 It's not known why she swallowed the fly.

In the deep structures underlying these examples, we may presume that the antecedent is a specific noun or pronoun; notice, for example, that 5.75 and 5.76 can be expressed equally well as:

5.81 Moneylenders generally know the ones who(m) they can trust to pay them back.

5.82 Fred often thinks about that which no one else is thinking about at the time.

In examples 5.77–5.80, we can posit the presence of the nouns *place, time, way,* and *reason*, respectively. In example 5.80, moreover, notice the fact that upon extraposition of the relative clause, the pronoun *it* has been left in the place of the original NP. The occurrence of *it* upon extraposition is thus governed by whether or not an entire NP has been moved, regardless of whether or not the clause constitutes the entire NP in deep structure.

MORE ON RELATIVE CLAUSE
TRANSFORMATIONS

In Chapter 4, it was noted that corresponding to each semantic-feature specification for a noun, for example [−Masculine], there is a corresponding selectional feature, for example [[−Masculine]___]. Now consider the following sentences:

5.83 I first met my wife in Boston.

5.84 Our chauffeur retired six months ago.

On the basis of the way in which sentences 5.83 and 5.84 are understood, we would want to maintain that they have the same deep structures as the following sentences:

5.85 I first met the one who is my wife in Boston.

5.86 The one who was our chauffeur retired six months ago.

But if we do so, then presumably the relative pronoun plus *be*-deletion transformation has applied in the case of 5.83 and 5.84, and another rule has applied to replace the pronoun *one* by the NP *my wife* and *our chauffeur*. Now, the pronoun *one*, in sentences 5.83 and 5.84 receives from the N *wife* the specification

[—Masculine], and when that N substitutes for that pronoun, as in 5.83, it may be supposed that it then takes on that specification. Suppose further that it could be shown that every occurrence of every noun in every deep structure of every sentence of English is as a predicate noun to some indefinite pronoun (say *one*, or *thing*), as in Bach (1968). Then we could hold that the entire semantic representation of nouns is in terms of selectional features, too, just like those of verbs and adjectives. Nouns would only take on feature specifications upon substitution for one or the other of the indefinite pronouns. This would effectively mean that as far as deep structures are concerned, the categorial distinction between nouns, verbs, and adjectives is irrelevant. These would be surface-structure distinctions only.

The position that every noun in English occurs as a predicate in deep structure receives empirical support from a variety of considerations. Consider a sentence such as the following, in which a prenominal modifier occurs which cannot be considered to arise from a deep-structure relative-clause construction:

5.87 The former king of Burundi is in exile.

Note that there is no sentence in English such as:

5.88 *The king of Burundi was former.

Sentence 5.87 can be construed, rather, to have a deep structure which is the same as that of:

5.89 The one who was formerly king of Burundi is in exile.

On the other hand, the ambiguity of a sentence such as:

5.90 The old chairman is still vigorous.

can be accounted for by presuming that two different deep structures underlie it, one being that of the sentence:

5.91 The chairman who is old is still vigorous.

and the other that of:

5.92 The one who of old was chairman is still vigorous.

Also the different ways of interpreting the NP *the Pope* in examples 2.22 and 2.23 can be explained with the help of this position; other problems with those sentences must also be dealt with, however, before a complete account can be given. These are taken up in Chapter 6.

Further support for the position under consideration is provided by the fact that sentences 5.93–5.94 below are ambiguous in a way that 5.95–5.96 are not:

5.93   Nicholas was a poor czar.
5.94   Ricky is a colorful cook.
5.95   Nicholas was a poor individual.
5.96   Ricky is a good-natured cook.

Example 5.93 means either that Nicholas was a poor person who was also a czar or that as a czar he did poorly, while 5.95 unambiguously asserts only that he was poverty-stricken (although the sentence could be interpreted in other ways, analogous to the second sense of 5.93, by stretching the sense of *individual* somewhat). Similarly, example 5.94 means either that Ricky is a colorful person who is a cook, or that as a cook he is colorful, while 5.96 only means that he is a good-natured person who is also a cook. The ambiguity of 5.93–5.94 can directly be accounted for by assuming that each has one deep structure in which *czar* and *cook* occur directly as predicates, and one in which the main predicate is an indefinite pronoun modified by two relative clauses, one containing the adjectives, and the other the nouns *czar* and *cook* as predicates. The unambiguity of 5.95 follows from the fact that it makes no difference semantically whether Nicholas was a poor one who was an individual or a poor individual, while that of 5.96 from the fact that *good-natured*, unlike colorful, is not a possible modifier of *cook* in deep structure.

   This last observation, incidentally, correlates with a subtle distinction in the use of the adverbs *colorfully* and *good-naturedly* when they modify the verb *cook*, as in the sentences:

5.97   Ricky cooks colorfully.
5.98   Ricky cooks good-naturedly.

In 5.97, the adverb qualifies the actions of Ricky's cooking, while in 5.98, it qualifies his attitudes while cooking. And in general it will be the case that when an adjective modifies a predicate noun which is in turn related to a verb, its sense will correspond to that of the *ly*-adverb which modifies the verb. Another example comparable to 5.94 is:

5.99   Martin is a brilliant actor.

The problem of adequately characterizing the deep structures of sentences like 5.93–5.97 is taken up again briefly in Chapter 6, footnote 2, and in the problems.

   This concludes our discussion of relative-clause formation. We shall deal with the remaining two topics in this chapter — pronominalization and conjunction — in somewhat less detail.

PRONOMINALIZATION TRANSFORMATIONS

In Chapter 2, passing reference was made to some intuitions that fluent speakers of English have concerning pronominalization, while in Chapter 4 it was noted that the transformational rules related to pronominalization must take into account the referential index of NP's. If we restrict our attention to the so-called third-person personal pronouns *he, she, it, they, him, her, them, his, its, their,* we may say that a pronoun substitutes for an NP under one of two conditions: (1) optionally in case the NP is coreferential with an NP following it in a sentence and the first NP is in a clause subordinate to the sentence containing the second NP. This situation is illustrated schematically in Fig. 5.23. Notice that this condition is fulfilled by the deep structure

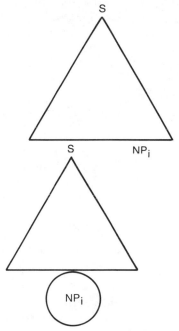

Fig. 5.23. Condition under which backwards pronominalization can take place to replace the circled NP by an appropriate pronoun.

that underlies sentence 2.25, which we repeat below for convenience. The pronominalization rule which has replaced the first occurrence of *Frank* by the pronoun *he* may be called *backwards pronominalization.*

5.100 (= **2.25**) After he₁ went to the movies last night, Frank₁ drove 150 miles to visit his₁ former college roommate.

The other condition is: (2) obligatorily in case the NP is coreferential with an NP preceding it in a sentence in which both occur, and optionally in case the NP preceding it is in a previous sentence of the discourse. This condition is fulfilled, for example, by the deep structure underlying sentence 4.38, which we repeat below.

5.101 (= **4.38**) The man₁ said that he₁ was coming.

This pronominalization rule may be called *forwards pronominalization*. The forwards pronominalization rule has also applied to sentence 5.100 to substitute the pronoun *his* for *Frank's*.

The order of application of the two rules of pronominalization is first backwards pronominalization and second forwards pronominalization, since if the backwards rule does not apply to a deep structure (recall that it is an optional transformation), then the forwards rule must apply. This accounts for the fact that the deep structure underlying sentence 5.100 could also be realized as:

5.102 After Frank₁ went to the movies last night, he₁ drove 150 miles to visit his₁ former college roommate.

The application of the backwards pronominalization rule crucially depends on the occurrence in a subordinate clause of the NP being pronominalized. It does not matter if the following coreferential NP is in another subordinate clause or not (just as long as it is not in the same clause as the first NP).⁸ Thus, for example, it is possible to obtain by backwards pronominalization such a sentence as the following:

5.103 The man who shot her₂ believed that there was someone else who was seeing Helen₂.

By extending somewhat the class of structures which satisfy the backwards pronominalization rule, it is possible to regard as a case of backwards pronominalization the replacement of a clause by *it* after it has been copied at the end of a sentence by the first step of the extraposition transformation. Recall that upon application of the first step of the rule of extraposition, a structure like that of Fig. 5.24 is obtained. Technically, the first NP in Fig. 5.24 is not contained in a subordinate clause, rather

---

⁸This account of pronominalization is based on the work of Ross (1967) and Langacker (forthcoming). For further consequences of and difficulties with this means of dealing with pronominalization, see the problems of Chapter 5.

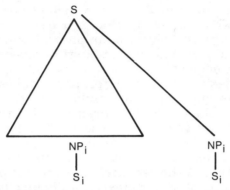

Fig. 5.24. Schematization of the structure resulting upon application of the first step of the extraposition transformation.

it *is* a subordinate clause. Also the rule which replaces it by the pronoun *it* is obligatory rather than optional. These differences, however, should not prevent us from considering the rule which effects this replacement as being a backwards pronominalization rule analogous to (but not identical with) the rule of the same name that we have been discussing.

In case the forwards pronominalization rule applies to replace an NP by a pronoun which is coreferential with an NP in the same clause (which may be the "main clause," that is, the sentence as a whole), then the pronoun comes out as a so-called REFLEXIVE PRONOUN, for example, *himself, herself, itself, themselves*. We can think of the reflexive form arising upon application of a reflexivization transformation which adds a reflexive feature to any pronoun which is coreferential with an NP in the same clause; this rule also applies in the case of so-called first- and second-person pronouns, as the following examples illustrate:

> **5.104** The man$_1$ reassured himself$_1$ that he$_1$ was in control of the situation.
>
> **5.105** You$_1$ will only injure yourself$_1$ if you$_1$ try to lift it by yourself$_1$.
>
> **5.106** I$_1$ thought that I$_1$ had behaved myself$_1$ well last night.

In example 5.104, the first but not the second occurrence of the pronoun is reflexivized since only it is in the same clause as the coreferential NP. In 5.105, each occurrence of *you* in each clause conditions an occurrence of *yourself* following it in each clause, while in 5.106, the reflexive pronoun *myself* occurs in the subordinate clause because a coreferential occurrence of *I* precedes it in that clause.

The verb *behave*, incidentally, which occurs in 5.106 is a reflexive verb, which is to say that if it occurs with an object at all, it occurs only with object noun phrases which are coreferential with its subject. It is an interesting question whether this is true at the deep-structure level, as well as at the point at which the reflexivization transformation takes place. In order to answer this question, one would have to ask whether the presence of an object NP coreferential with the subject NP of *behave* serves any semantic purpose. If it does not, then, presumably, *behave* is to be considered an intransitive verb, but one which requires that its subject NP be copied as its object prior to the application of the reflexivization transformation.

The presence of the reflexive pronouns *yourself* or *yourselves* in certain imperative sentences, for example:

5.107 Behave yourself this evening.

is convincing syntactic evidence that in the deep structure of such sentences the NP *you* (or any NP coreferential with *you*—see Thorne [1966]) occurs as subject, which is not deleted transformationally until the reflexivization transformation has applied.

Similarly, notice the occurrence of reflexive pronouns in such sentences as:

5.108 The general expected himself to be killed by nightfall.

5.109 We consider ourselves to be the only possessors of truth.

Examples such as these provide the convincing evidence that the infinitival clause separation transformation applies as we described it in section 3 of this chapter to object infinitival clauses. The fact that reflexive pronouns are found in examples 5.108 and 5.109 means that the subjects of the infinitival clauses are also constituents of the main clauses (that is, the direct objects of the verbs *expect* and *consider*) at the point at which the reflexivization transformation applies. On the other hand, we know that in the deep structures underlying these sentences, this is not the case. Therefore a transformation is required to convert the subjects of the infinitival clauses in these sentences into the direct objects of the verbs *expect* and *believe*. The infinitival clause separation transformation is precisely the transformation needed to do the job. All we need to assume is that this transformation applies prior to the application of the reflexivization transformation.

Care, however, needs to be exercised in the exact formulation of the infinitival clause separation transformation, for consider now the sentence:

5.110 The teacher expected the class to take care of itself.

From sentence 5.110, we find that at the point of application of the reflexivization transformation, the subject of the infinitive must also be a constituent of the infinitival clause; otherwise we would not expect to find the reflexive pronoun *itself* occurring as it does in example 5.110. The conclusion that we must draw from this example and from examples 5.108-5.109 is that at the point of application of the reflexivization transformation, the subject of an object infinitival clause is *simultaneously* the subject of the clause and the direct object of the verb in the main clause. This means that the infinitival-clause separation transformation does not apply exactly as we indicated in Figs. 5.3-5.6, but rather as in Figs. 5.25-5.30. The first step of the

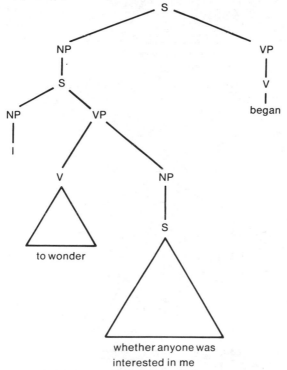

Fig. 5.25 (= Fig. 5.3). Deep structure of sentence 5.14.

transformation copies both the subject and the predicate of the infinitival clause as constituents of the main clause, as indicated in Figs. 5.26 and 5.29. The second step deletes the original infinitival clause entirely, resulting in surface structures as depicted in Figs. 5.27 and 5.30. The reflexivization transformation,

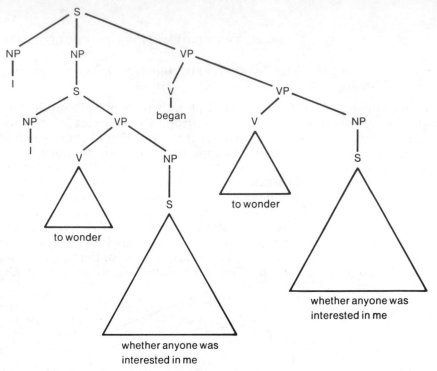

Fig. 5.26. First step of the infinitival clause separation transformation applied to the deep structure of sentence 5.14.

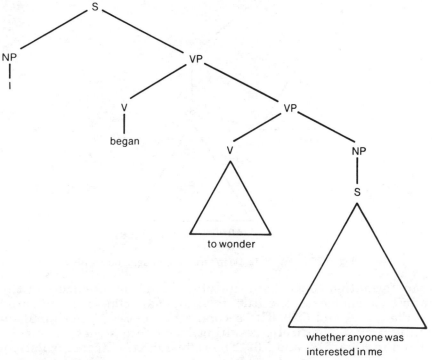

Fig. 5.27 (= Fig. 5.4). Surface structure of sentence 5.14, resulting from the second step in the application of the infinitival clause separation transformation.

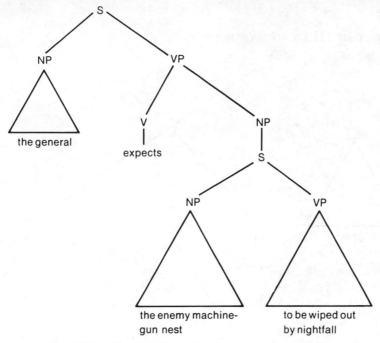

Fig. 5.28 (= Fig. 5.5). Deep structure of sentence 5.15.

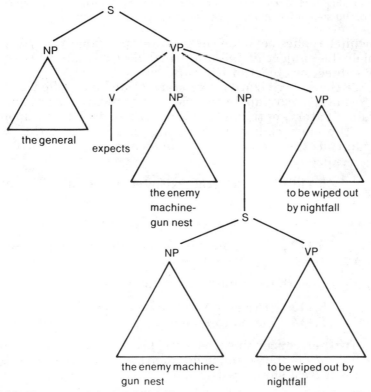

Fig. 5.29. First step of the infinitival clause separation transformation applied to the deep structure of sentence 5.15.

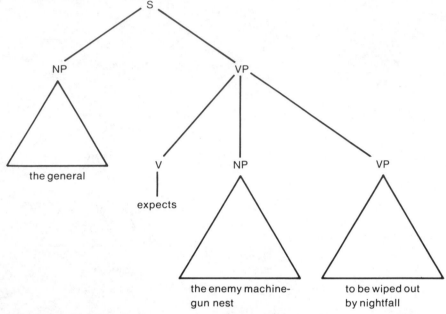

Fig. 5.30 (= Fig. 5.6). Surface structure of sentence 5.16, resulting from application of the second step of the infinitival clause separation transformation.

meanwhile, applies between these two steps; namely, at the point at which the subject of the infinitival clause exists as such and as the subject or object of the main clause.

After the reflexivization transformation has applied, another transformation may apply to delete the reflexive pronoun. This rule is obligatory, optional, or inapplicable, depending upon the verb in the main clause. In case the verb is *expect*, the rule is optional; thus the deep structure underlying sentence 5.108 may also be realized as:

> **5.111** The general expected to be killed by nightfall.

whereas following the verb *consider*, the rule is inapplicable:

> **5.112** *We consider to be the only possessors of truth.

Following the verb *try*, finally, the rule is obligatory:

> **5.113** *I tried myself to be honest.
> **5.114** I tried to be honest.

Notice further concerning the verb *try*, that the subject of its object infinitival clause must be identical with its own subject; this is a feature it shares with such verbs as *confess*.

We conclude this discussion of pronominalization in English by pointing out the fact that two sentences may have almost identical surface structures but almost entirely different deep structures. Compare sentence 5.114, for example, with:

5.115 I began to be honest.

which differ in surface structure only in that where 5.114 has the verb *tried*, 5.115 has the verb *began*. Sentence 5.114, however, has the deep structure as illustrated in Fig. 5.31, in which *I* occurs as the deep-structure subject and an infinitival clause as object, whereas sentence 5.115 has the deep structure as illustrated in Fig. 5.32, in which there is no direct object and which an infinitival clause serves as subject.[9]

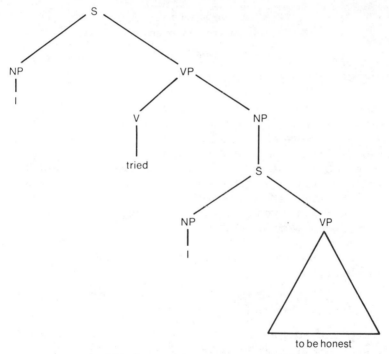

Fig. 5.31. Deep structure of sentence 5.114.

---

[9]Note that any NP can occur as the surface subject of a verb such as *begin*, but that only animate subjects occur with *try* without there being an internal contradiction. Compare the sentences:

   (i)   There began to be a shortage of water in New York.
   (ii) There tried to be a shortage of water in New York.
and
   (iii) The building began to collapse.
   (iv) The building tried to collapse.

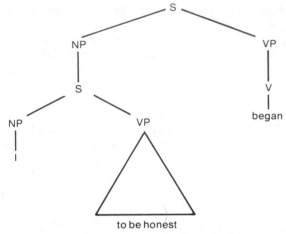

Fig. 5.32. Deep structure of sentence 5.115.

CONJUNCTION REDUCTION TRANSFORMATIONS

The last topic to be dealt with in this chapter relates to conjunction. Whenever two or more sentences are conjoined and share one or more constituents, then generally in the surface structure of these conjoined sentences there is only one occurrence of the shared constituents. Examples 2.40 and 3.55 are illustrative. Clearly a transformational rule is needed to eliminate all but one of the occurrences of these shared constituents. Without describing yet how such a rule must work, we may give it a name, CONJUNCTION REDUCTION.

To see how conjunction reduction must operate, let us consider first the deep and surface structures of example 3.55, which we repeat here:

> **5.116 (= 3.55)** President Johnson and Secretary McNamara flew to Guam.

The deep and surface structures of this example are given in Figs. 5.33 and 5.34, respectively. From consideration of these structures, it is clear that the application of conjunction reduction does not simply involve deleting the predicate of the second conjunct. Such an operation would indeed eliminate one of the shared predicates, but it would leave us with an incorrect surface structure, namely that given in Fig. 5.35 (we assume the application of a transformation to move the conjunction to its position in surface structures). In order to obtain the correct surface structure for sentence 5.116, we need first to copy the shared predicate as a constituent of the sentence as a whole. The effect of this step is to produce the structure shown in Fig.

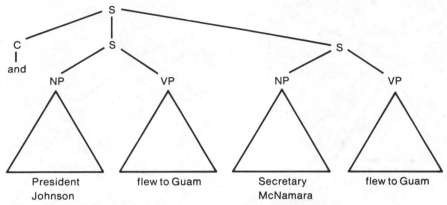

Fig. 5.33. Deep structure for sentence 5.116.

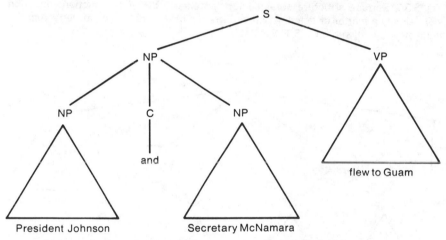

Fig. 5.34. Surface structure for sentence 5.116.

5.36. The second step is then to eliminate both occurrences of the predicate in the conjoined sentences, along with the constituents circled in Fig. 5.36, the result being that shown in Fig. 5.37. The third step involves "creating" a constituent NP to include the conjunction *and* and the two NP's. This is a completely ad hoc step, but there does not appear to be any alternative within this framework. In any event, the result of this third step is the surface structure of sentence 5.116 as depicted in Fig. 5.34.

As another illustration of conjunction reduction, consider the sentence:

      5.117 Grandma drinks seltzer and smokes Havana cigars.

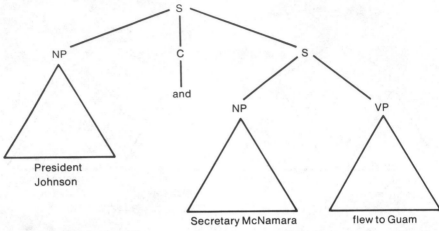

Fig. 5.35. Surface structure obtained for sentence 5.116 if conjunction reduction were simply a matter of deleting one occurrence of the shared constituent from the deep structure of sentence 5.116.

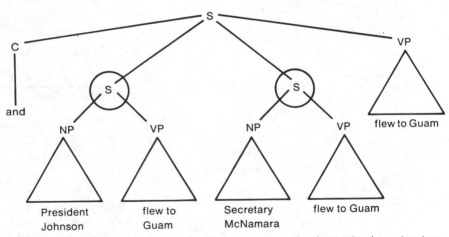

Fig. 5.36. First step in the application of conjunction reduction to the deep structure of sentence 5.116.

whose surface structure contains a conjoined predicate. The deep structure of sentence 5.117 is given in Fig. 5.38. The successive applications of the steps of the conjunction reduction transformation to it are indicated in Figs. 5.39–5.41.

In 5.116 and 5.117, the shared constituents of the conjoined sentences are found at one end or the other of those sentences. In case the shared constituents occur in the middle of each con-

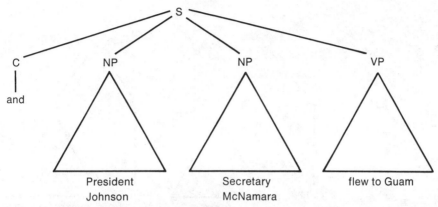

Fig. 5.37. Second step in the application of conjunction reduction to the deep structure of sentence 5.116.

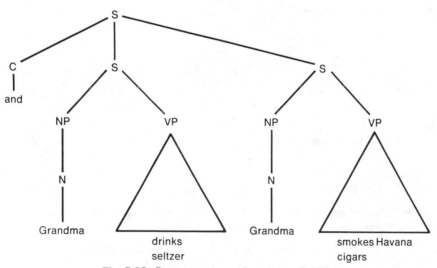

Fig. 5.38. Deep structure of sentence 5.117.

junct, then conjunction reduction can be viewed simply as a transformation which deletes the second occurrence of that constituent. Sentence 5.118 illustrates this situation:

> **5.118** Harry watches the fights and his wife the soap operas.

Conjunction reduction, however, may involve pronominalization as well as deletion of shared constituents. It is claimed that

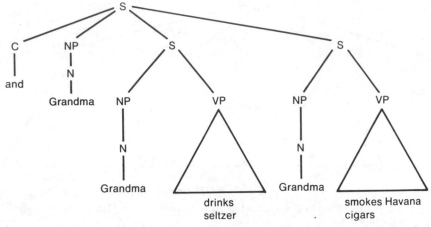

Fig. 5.39. First step in the application of conjunction reduction to the deep structure of sentence 5.117.

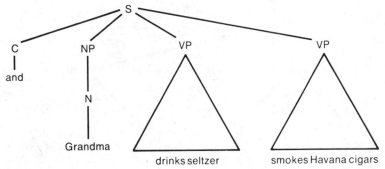

Fig. 5.40. Second step in the application of conjunction reduction to the deep structure of sentence 5.117.

the following sentences are all obtainable from the same deep structure:

 5.119 Harry and his wife watch the fights.
 5.120 Harry watches the fights and his wife watches them, too.
 5.121 Harry watches the fights and so does his wife.

Detailed consideration of these and other problems involving conjunction reduction would, however, take up too much space here and would involve us in extremely complex arguments. For a treatment of these matters from a somewhat different perspective, see Gleitman (1965). We now pass on to other syntactic problems related to conjunction.

 Earlier in our discussion of relative-clause formation, we

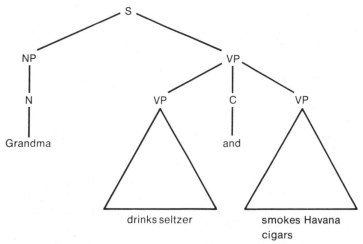

Fig. 5.41. Third step, resulting in the surface structure of sentence 5.117.

observed that there are two kinds of relative clauses in English, one which we set off in writing by commas and one which we do not. These two are illustrated for us in the following sentences:

> **5.122** The Chinese, who are industrious, control the economy of Singapore.
> **5.123** The Chinese who are industrious control the economy of Singapore.

The relative clause in example 5.122 is known as a NONRESTRICTIVE, or APPOSITIVE, RELATIVE CLAUSE, while that in 5.123 is known as a RESTRICTIVE RELATIVE CLAUSE. Nonrestrictive relative clauses are not felt to be subordinate to the nouns they occur with, but rather coordinate. Thus sentence 5.122 is not interpreted to mean anything different from the sentence:

> **5.124** The Chinese are industrious, and they control the economy of Singapore.

If we postulate the same deep structure for sentences 5.122 and 5.124, then presumably there is an optional apposition transformation which converts the first conjunct into a nonrestrictive relative clause modifying the shared NP in the second conjunct.[10]

Despite the deep-structure differences between example 5.122 and 5.123, however, the relative pronoun plus *be*-deletion transformation is satisfied by both of them (the apposition trans-

---

[10]As we can now see, Jespersen (1969) was mistaken to view extraposition and apposition as the same process. The only thing they have in common is that they both move clauses around.

formation must first apply to the structure underlying 5.122, of course), and if it is applied, then the adjective *industrious* must be preposed to the noun. The result in both cases is the sentence[11]:

5.125 The industrious Chinese control the economy of Singapore.

Unlike deep-structure conjunction of sentences, deep-structure conjunction of noun phrases does not lead to the consequent application of rules of conjunction reduction. However, NP conjunction does involve us in transformational rules of a different sort. There are certain verbs and nouns which seemingly occur with a subject and an object such that if you interchange subject and object, no significant change in meaning ensues. For example, consider the sentences:

5.126 The tanker collided with the steamer.
5.127 The steamer collided with the tanker.
5.128 Pauline is married to Harvey.
5.129 Harvey is married to Pauline.
5.130 This sample is similar to that one.
5.131 That sample is similar to this one.
5.132 My opinion differs slightly from yours.
5.133 Your opinion differs slightly from mine.
5.134 The foreign secretary is a relative of the home secretary.
5.135 The home secretary is a relative of the foreign secretary.

The verbs, adjectives, and nouns occurring in 5.126–5.135, *collide, married, similar, differ,* and *relative,* among others that have the same property, may be called SYMMETRIC PREDICATES. They also have the property that the interchangeable NP's can also occur conjoined as their subjects, thus[12]:

---

[11]Example 5.125 is only ambiguous in writing however, not in speech. If *industrious* comes from a deep structure restrictive relative clause, then the adjective is stressed, while if it comes from a nonrestrictive relative clause, then the noun is stressed.

[12]Some of the examples below are ambiguous; thus for example 5.137 means either that Pauline and Harvey are husband and wife or that simply each one is married, not necessarily to each other. The latter interpretation arises from conjunction reduction from the conjoined sentences:

   (i) Pauline is married and Harvey is married.

   It is possible to maintain, moreover, as does Gleitman (1965), that sentences such as 5.136 arise from conjunction reduction of sentences such as 5.126 and 5.127 taken together. The first step in the conjunction reduction of:

   (ii) The tanker collided with the steamer and the steamer collided with the tanker.
would be:

   (iii) The tanker and the steamer collided with each other.

5.136 The tanker and the steamer collided.
5.137 Pauline and Harvey are married.
5.138 This sample and that one are similar.
5.139 My opinion and yours differ slightly.
5.140 The foreign secretary and the home secretary are relatives.

When the noun phrases occur as conjoined subjects, similarly no change in meaning is obtained if they are interchanged:

5.141 The steamer and the tanker collided.

The fact that sentences containing symmetric predicates have essentially the same meaning regardless of whether their noun phrases occur as conjoined subjects or separately as subject and object, and regardless of the order in which the noun phrases occur, would suggest that the same deep structure underlies them all. In particular, suppose we take sentences 5.126 and 5.136 as having the same deep structure. Then where do the noun phrases occur in that deep structure? The answer would seem to be that they occur as conjoined noun phrases, since it would be an arbitrary decision to identify one as subject and the other as object. To obtain the surface structure of 5.126, however, a transformation would be required to copy the second conjunct as the object of the symmetric predicate, and some decision would have to be made to insure that the appropriate preposition (*to, with, from, of*) is selected to precede it. The problem of the choice of preposition is not as easy as it would seem at first glance (the problem is taken up further in Chapter 6), but assuming that some solution to it is possible, then the syntactic facts concerning symmetric predicates can be accounted for satisfactorily.

A subsequent transformational rule is then required to delete, optionally, *with each other*, resulting in 5.136. One difficulty with this approach is that the putative preposition plus *each other*-deletion transformation would have to "know" whether the verb, adjective, or noun preceding the expression to be deleted was a symmetric predicate or not. Thus from the conjoined sentences:

(iv)   Fred listened to Tony and Tony listened to Fred.
we obtain:

(v)   Fred and Tony listened to each other.
but not (with the same meaning):

(vi)   Fred and Tony listened.

6 ENGLISH SENTENCE TYPES

In this chapter we provide a very sketchy account of the grammatical properties of various TYPES of English sentences. What we mean by type will become clear as we proceed. However, before we can begin with the presentation, a reconsideration of the constituent-structure rules which govern the formation of deep structures is called for. In Chapters 3–5 we raised two important objections to the deep-structure rules formulated in Chapter 3: (1) that they obscure the underlying relationships between verbs and adjectives and NP's, and (2) that they make a categorical distinction between nouns, verbs, and adjectives which does not appear to be necessary in deep structure.

These objections could be met if the rules of constituent structure for the formation of sentences differed from that of 3.58. First rule 3.58(a), which analyzes sentences into subjects and predicates, and rules 3.58(f–g), which analyze predicates into verbs and objects, or simply as verbs, must be dropped. In their place, we require a rule which analyzes sentences as consisting of a verb, adjective, or noun, together with one, two, or possibly three noun phrases. Now, since the term "predicate" has been freed from its old usage as the name for the relation holding between a verb phrase and the sentence containing it, we may use that term instead as the name for the grammatical category consisting of verbs, adjectives, and nouns (abbreviated P). Notice that in Chapter 5 we already made use of the term in the way we have just defined it, namely in our discussion of symmetric predicates; this usage of the term is moreover standard in the field of logic. The designation of a lexical item as a noun, verb, or adjective is to be done in terms of syntactic features.[1]

Also, rules 3.58(b,d,e) must be eliminated—3.58(c,h,i), however, remain. Rules 3.58(b,d) are replaced by rules which analyze noun phrases as consisting either of an INDEFINITE PRONOUN (abbreviated IP) or of an indefinite pronoun and a sentence. The inventory of rules of deep constituent structure may therefore be stated as in 6.1:

6.1 (a) $S \rightarrow P\ NP^n$ ($n = 1, 2, 3$)
   (b) $S \rightarrow C\ S^*$
   (c) $NP \rightarrow C\ NP^*$
   (d) $NP \rightarrow IP$
   (e) $NP \rightarrow IP\ S$
   (f) $NP \rightarrow S$

According to rule 6.1(a), a sentence may consist of a predicate and from one to three noun phrases. We call a predicate which occurs with one NP a *one-place* predicate, one which occurs with two noun phrases a *two-place* predicate, and one with three noun phrases a *three-place* predicate, and the noun phrases are called the ARGUMENTS of these predicates. One-place predicates correspond to the former notion of intransitive verbs or nouns and two-place predicates to that of transitive verbs and nouns. Three-place predicates correspond to nothing we have dealt with in the preceding chapters, but the reader should have no trouble recognizing that certain verbs stand in a relationship with three arguments, two of which in traditional grammar are called objects. Examples of three-place predicates in English are the verbs *show*, *strike*, and *tell*, which occur as such in the sentences:

6.2 I showed the class my collection of buttons.
6.3 The bullet struck the governor in the thigh.
6.4 Your best friends won't tell you that you have bad breath.

Rules 6.1(b,c) are, as before, the rules which govern sentence and noun-phrase coordination. Rule 6.1(d) permits an NP to consist solely of an indefinite pronoun, which we may take to be the lexical items *one* (with the semantic specification [+Human]) and *that* (with the specification [−Human]), while rule 6.1(e) permits a NP to have also a relative clause. Finally rule 6.1(f) allows an NP to consist solely of a sentence.

---

[1]For important discussions of the nature of the noun/verb/adjective distinction in general and in various languages, see the work of B. L. Whorf in Carroll (1956), especially pp. 215–216.

If the rules of 6.1 are taken to be the rules of deep-structure formation, then the selection of an argument as subject of a sentence becomes the task of a transformational rule. In a sentence containing a one-place predicate, the task of the subjectivization transformation is obvious: it takes the single argument of the predicate and copies it in front of the predicate, deleting it in its original position. In case we are given a two- or three-place predicate, then a selection has to be made of the argument which is to become the surface-structure subject. In case an argument is present upon which the predicate has imposed the specifications that it is animate and an agent (intuitively, the one who carries out the action of the predicate), then that argument is made subject, as in, for examples, 6.2-6.4. If there is no such argument, then other conditions of selection may apply or there may be freedom of selection. Consider, for example, the deep structure in which the two-place predicate *dissolve* appears together with an argument designating location, for example *in the innocent-looking acid* and an argument designating a [3 Penetrable] substance, for example *the metal*. Then either argument may be made the surface-structure subject of the sentence, and one of them must be; in other words we have both:

6.5 (= 3.23) The innocent-looking acid dissolved the metal.

and:

6.6 (= 3.24) The metal dissolved in the innocent-looking acid.

Before we can exhibit any deep structures constructed in accordance with the rules of 6.1, however, we need to deal with some special properties of a particular predicate, namely *be*. It turns out, first of all, that predicates identifiable as surface-structure nouns and adjectives do not occur in deep structures except when they are contained within a sentence which functions as one of the arguments of the predicate *be*. This is a complicated way of saying that such predicates only occur in configurations such as that indicated in Fig. 6.1. Let us first consider adjectives. We have already observed that adjectives occur in surface structures following a form of the predicate *be* unless that form has been transformationally deleted. Ross (1967), however, in order to account for the occurrence of the pronouns italicized in the following and in similar examples, observed further that adjectives must be considered to occur inside noun phrases:

6.7 Claude is intelligent, but he hardly looks *it*.
6.8 Mary is outspoken, *which* is *what* Martha is, too.

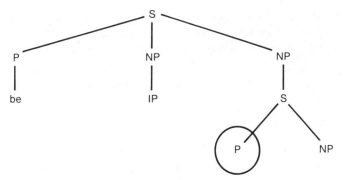

Fig. 6.1 Predicates identifiable as nouns or adjectives occur only in deep-structure configurations like this one, in the position of the circled P.

This means that we must provide a sentence such as:

6.9 One is intelligent.

with a deep structure something like that shown in Fig. 6.2. To

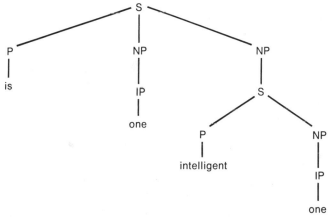

Fig. 6.2. Deep structure of sentence 6.9.

obtain the surface structure of sentence 6.9, the subjectiviza-tion transformation must apply and also a rule very much like the infinitival-clause separation transformation of Chapter 5 (the subordinate clause in Fig. 6.2 can be considered to be a kind of infinitival clause; note also that we no longer provide for a constituent named VP, so that the infinitival-clause separation transformation will in any event have to be revised if the rules of 6.1 are adopted), to convert the adjective *intelligent* into a constituent of the main clause. The reflexive deletion transfor-mation will then get rid of the extra occurrence of the IP.

Similar evidence can be used to show that a predicate noun must also occur within a sentence which functions as an argument of the predicate *be*. For example, notice the use of the italicized pronouns in the following examples (particularly note that the pronoun *it* and *what* occur, not *he* and *who*):

> **6.10** Claude is a man, but he hardly looks *it*.
> **6.11** Percy is a song-writer, *which* is *what* Marvin is, too.

This means that the deep structure for the sentence:

> **6.12** One is a man.

must be something like that shown in Fig. 6.3 (again we ignore the problem posed by the article *a*). If we make the assumption

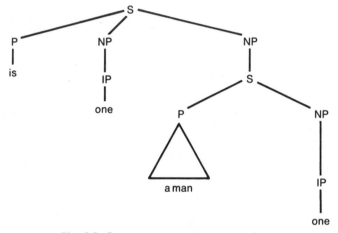

Fig. 6.3. Deep structure of sentence 6.12.

that proper names are predicates, too, just like ordinary nouns, then the deep structure for a sentence such as:

> **6.13** Claude is a man.

can be represented as in Fig. 6.4. One obtains the surface structure of 6.13 from its deep structure in exactly the same way in which one obtains the surface structure of 6.12 from its deep structure. The subjectivization transformation applies, moving the first argument to the left of the *is* in the main clause; it also applies in the various subordinate clauses. A version of the infinitival clause separation transformation then applies, and ultimately the "subjects" of the predicates *a man* and *Claude* are eliminated. The relative pronoun formation transformation has meanwhile applied. Then, upon deletion of the relative pronoun plus *is*, the predicate *Claude* substitutes for the subject IP *one*, and the surface structure of sentence 6.13 is obtained. Ad-

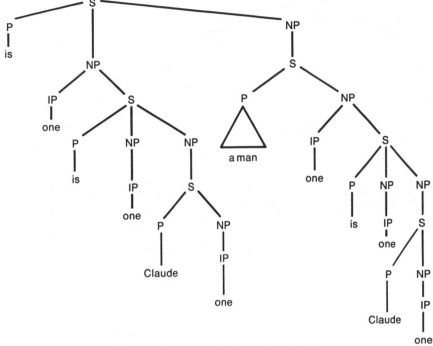

Fig. 6.4. Deep structure of sentence 6.13.

mittedly, it is an indication of the abstractness of the deep structure underlying sentence 6.11 that it contains six occurrences of
the indefinite pronoun and five subordinate clauses, whereas the
surface structure of the sentence has none of either. But only
something so abstract can possibly serve as a representation of
how a sentence such as 6.13 is understood intuitively by fluent
speakers of English. Deep structures for sentences whose surface structures are more complex than that of 6.13 will look even
more abstract than this one.[2] In particular consider the deep

[2] Consider, for example, what the deep structures for examples 5.93–5.96 would have to contain in order to make provision for the observations made in the discussion concerning
those examples. One of the interesting consequences of those observations is that the indefinite pronouns, which we have taken to constitute a separate category in English, are
themselves predicates, but that when they occur as predicates, they are obligatorily modified by at least one relative clause! This last proviso is required, since indefinite pronouns
never occur as surface structure predicates, but are always replaced by a predicate noun
from a relative clause. In order to avoid having to say that the head constituents of NP's
are designated members of the category predicate, we can, if we wish, replace every occurrence of IP in the rules of 6.1 by one of the symbols x, y, z, and so forth, and maintain
that every occurrence of one of these symbols, except as the argument of an indefinite
pronoun, is obligatorily accompanied by at least one relative clause. One function of these
symbols which, following the standard terminology of logic may be called VARIABLES, is to
indicate the reference, if any, of the nouns ultimately substituted for them.

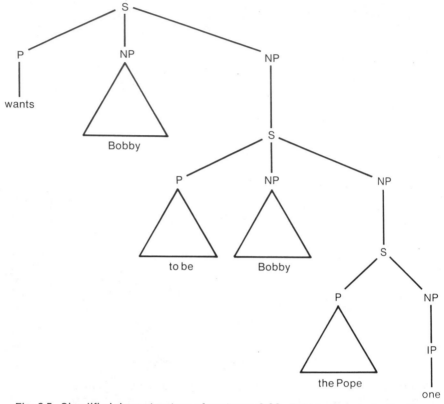

Fig. 6.5. Simplified deep structure of sentence 2.22: *Bobby wants to be the Pope.*

structures which we need to postulate to account for the difference in interpretation between sentences 2.22 and 2.23. Omitting
some details, those deep structures will have to look something
like those given in Figs. 6.5 and 6.6.

Now let us return to the problem of the relationship between
arguments and predicates in general. We may assume that each
predicate is strictly subcategorized according to the number of
arguments it has and that each one contains selectional features
to indicate what features are imposed on these arguments. Certain of these features are manifested not only by the head noun
of these arguments, but also by prepositions that may occur
with them. In an interesting series of papers, Fillmore (1966,
1968) has argued that such prepositions are best considered to
be constituents of the noun phrases with which they occur; in
fact, that prepositions are constituents of every deep-structure
argument, and that whenever a preposition fails to turn up in
a surface-structure argument, it has been transformationally
deleted. In English, the preposition of a subjectivized argument

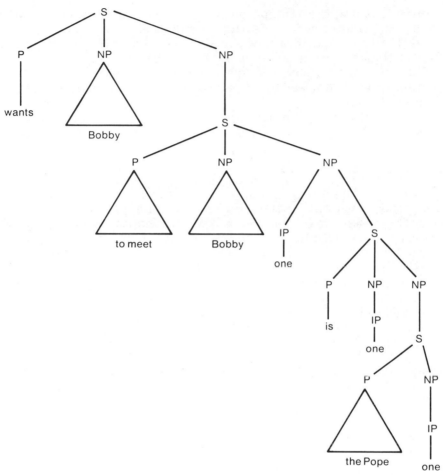

Fig. 6.6. Simplified deep structure of sentence 2.23: *Bobby wants to meet the Pope.*

is obligatorily deleted, while the preposition of the argument
which immediately follows a verb may or may not be deleted,
depending upon the verb (the preposition of an argument which
follows a noun or an adjective is never deleted). The preposition is moreover always deleted when the argument is simply
a sentence. Fillmore also noted a connection between certain
of the prepositions and features of the nouns which occur with
them; for example, the preposition that expresses agency, *by*,
occurs only with animate nouns. To complicate matters further,
however, certain of the prepositions, for example, *behind, about*,
and perhaps even all of them, must themselves be considered
to be predicates which take two arguments.

Rather than take up these matters in detail here, we shall

simply assume that the preposition associated with each argument contributes certain feature specifications to that argument
and that these specifications are also imposed by the verbs which
select that argument. Thus a verb like *dissolve* imposes on one
of its arguments, say, the specification [+Locative], a specification which is marked by the preposition *in* associated with that
argument.

Now let us consider once again sentences 3.19 and 3.20, which
we repeat here for convenience:

6.14 (= 3.19) The tree shook.
6.15 (= 3.20) The boy shook the tree.

In terms of the concepts of this chapter, the questions concerning these sentences that we asked in Chapter 3 can now be
worded as follows: how are the relationships between the predicate *shake* and its arguments to be stated, and is the predicate
shake with one argument the same lexical item as the predicate *shake* with two arguments?

In order to answer these questions satisfactorily, it is important to bear in mind the fact that example 6.15 has virtually
the same meaning as:

6.16 The boy caused the tree to shake.

Upon subjectivalization, example 6.16 has the structure depicted
in Fig. 6.7. We could account for the semantic relationship be-

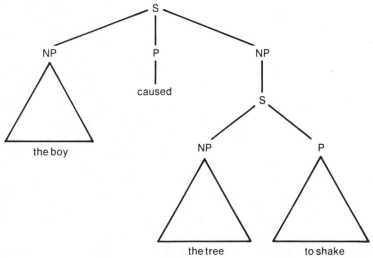

Fig. 6.7. Structure of sentence 6.16 upon application of the subjectivalization transformation.

tween 6.15 and 6.16 if we were to establish a deep structure for sentence 6.15 which is significantly similar to that which we provide for 6.16. Such a structure is indicated in Fig. 6.8 (once again we assume application of subjectivalization). The labeled

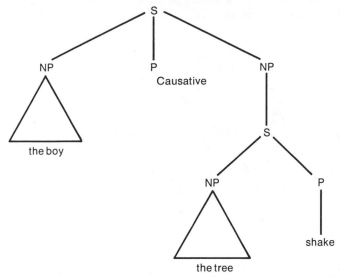

Fig. 6.8. Possible structure of sentence 6.15 upon application of subjectivalization.

predicate in Fig. 6.8 represents a verb with the same selectional features as the verb *cause*, but not associated with any particular lexical item. We call this predicate, following Lakoff (1965), an ABSTRACT CAUSATIVE PREDICATE. To obtain the surface structure of sentence 6.15, a transformational rule is required which simply substitutes the predicate *shake* for the abstract predicate, thus accounting for how the verb *shake* takes on a causative meaning in that sentence. We are also enabled to say that *shake* is a single lexical item which occurs in deep structure with just one argument. In the same way we can consider such predicates as *break*, *open*, *grow*, and the like to be lexical items which occur with one argument in deep structure. We can say that when they occur in sentences with two arguments, one of them being an agent NP, they have replaced the abstract causative predicate.

By similar reasoning we can establish the existence of an abstract instrumental predicate. Consider the following sentences, for example:

6.17 The carpenter used the hammer to strike the nail.

6.18 The carpenter struck the nail with the hammer.

Let us suppose that the verb *use* is a three-place predicate, whose arguments are an agent, an instrument, and an infinitival clause expressing what may be called result. Following Fillmore, we associate the preposition *by* with the agent NP and *with* with the instrumental NP. Thus, sentence 6.17 receives roughly the deep structure given in Fig. 6.9. Upon application of the sub-

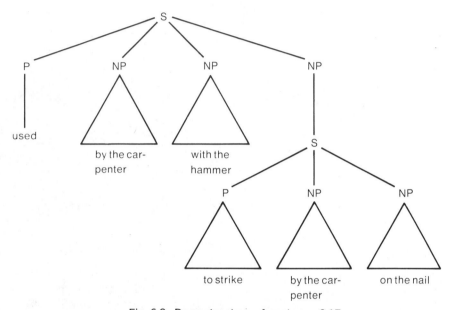

Fig. 6.9. Deep structure of sentence 6.17.

jectivalization transformation, the infinitival clause and reflexive pronoun deletion transformations, and a transformation to delete *with* following the verb *use*, the surface structure of sentence 6.17 follows directly from the deep structure depicted in Fig. 6.9.

In sentence 6.18, the verb *strike* is being used instrumentally; therefore we suggest that the structure illustrated in Fig. 6.10 is the deep structure of example 6.18; in Fig. 6.10 we have labeled the ABSTRACT INSTRUMENTAL PREDICATE as such. After application of the subjectivalization transformation, the predicate *strike* is substituted for the abstract predicate, and attracts to it the locative argument *on the nail*. Now, since the preposition *on* follows the verb, it is deleted, whereas *with* is retained, resulting in the surface structure of sentence 6.17.

As an aside concerning the predicate *strike* and similar predicates such as *hit*, *bump*, and *smash*, we note that noninstru-

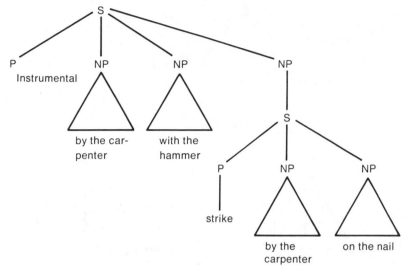

Fig. 6.10. Deep structure of sentence 6.18.

mental sentences containing them are generally ambiguous. For example:

6.19 The carpenter struck the nail.
6.20 George just bumped into an old lady carrying her groceries.

are interpreted in such a way that the surface subject may be either an agent NP or what Fillmore calls a dative NP, signifying one to whom something is felt to happen. It is interesting to note that *hit* and *strike* also select a somewhat different set of arguments, in which the locative NP is animate:

6.21 A clever idea struck me the other day.

The presence of an abstract predicate need not add arguments, as do the causative and instrumental abstract predicates. Consider the following pair of sentences:

6.22 The sky became dark.
6.23 The sky darkened.

The deep structure of sentence 6.22 is as in Fig. 6.11. On the basis of the similarity of the meaning of sentence 6.23 to that of 6.22, we can postulate a deep structure for 6.23 which contains an abstract predicate, which again following Lakoff (1965), we will call inchoative (technically this term means expressing the beginning of an action, a meaning which makes it not entirely appropriate). When a predicate is substituted for the ABSTRACT

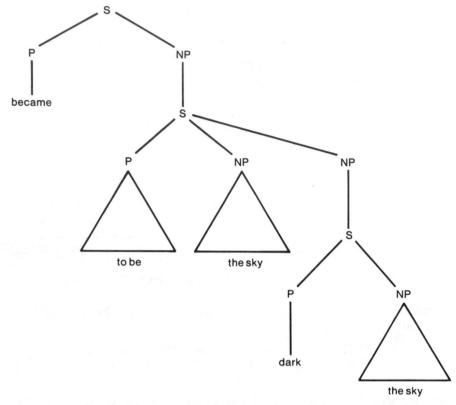

Fig. 6.11. Deep structure of sentence 6.22.

INCHOATIVE PREDICATE, moreover, it may undergo a change in form; thus *dark* becomes *darken.* The deep structure for sentence 6.23 is given in Fig. 6.12. Other predicates change in the same way as *dark* when they substitute for the abstract inchoative predicate; for example, *soft, hard, thick, red,* and *black* become *soften, harden, thicken, redden,* and *blacken,* respectively. Still others change in different ways; for example *hot, long,* and *solid* become *heat, lengthen,* and *solidify,* respectively; still others undergo no change at all; for example *yellow, warm,* and *cool* remain *yellow, warm,* and *cool.* The rules which govern the changes (if any) which lexical items undergo when they substitute for the abstract inchoative predicate will be discussed briefly in Chapter 7.

Now consider the sentence:

6.24 The chef heated the soup.

The fact that this sentence is paraphrasable as[3]:

6.25 The chef caused the soup to become hot.

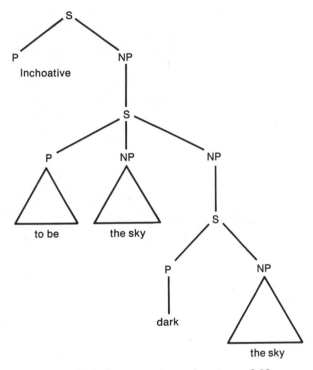

Fig. 6.12. Deep structure of sentence 6.23.

suggests that the deep structure contains both the causative and the inchoative abstract predicates. Such a deep structure is given in Fig. 6.13. To obtain the surface structure of 6.25, the adjective *hot* is first substituted for the inchoative predicate, becoming *heat*. This is in turn substituted for the causative predicate.

In an unpublished paper, Lakoff and Ross have presented interesting evidence that the deep structure for sentences like 6.24 must contain at least the abstract causative predicate having an argument consisting of a sentence. They point out that in a sentence such as:

6.26 The chef heated the soup, but it took him a long time to bring *it* about.

the antecedent to the underlined pronoun can only be the deep-structure sentential NP *the soup heat*. But for this to be so, that

---

[3] Example 6.25 is actually a paraphrase of only one sense of 6.24; the latter sentence can also be interpreted to mean simply that the chef caused the soup to become hotter than it was, but not necessarily hot in an absolute sense. See Problem 11 of Chapter 6 for further consideration of this matter.

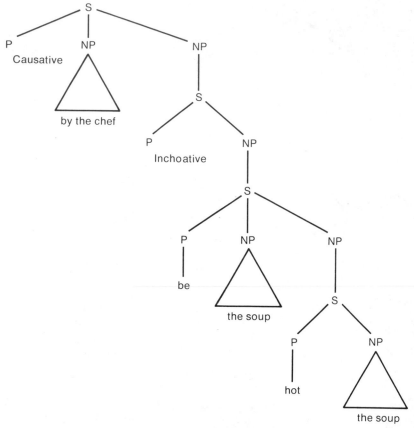

Fig. 6.13. Deep structure of sentence 6.24.

NP must appear in the deep structure in the initial clause *the chef heated the soup*.

Another argument which can be advanced to substantiate the same point is based on sentences such as:

6.27 The State Highway Department closed all the mountain passes in the northern part of the state until next spring.

Ordinarily, past-tense forms of verbs (for example, *closed*) do not occur in the same clause with future adverbial expressions (for example, *until next spring*); it is contradictory to say:

6.28   I wrote the book until next spring.

If, however, in sentence 6.27, we assume that *close* has substituted for the abstract causative predicate, then the adverbial *until next spring* can be viewed as a constituent of the clause subordinate to that predicate.

This completes our reconsideration of the constituent-structure rules which form the basis for the construction of deep structures, and we turn now to a consideration of the various types of English sentences. As it turns out, typological classification of the sentences of a language must proceed along several dimensions simultaneously. Two dimensions are immediately provided for by the constituent-structure rules 6.1: (1) the number of arguments of the predicate of the sentence, and (2) the kinds of features the predicate imposes on those arguments. Thus, sentences with one-, two-, and three-place predicates would belong to different types along the first dimension, while predicates which select agentive arguments, say, as opposed to dative arguments would belong to different types along the second dimension. As a special case of the second dimension, we can say that sentences whose main predicate is an abstract predicate of a certain kind constitute a sentence type—for example, the class of all sentences with the abstract inchoative predicate.

Of course, if we simply consider the surface structure of a sentence, we may have little evidence to go on as to what type it belongs to; what must be considered, rather, are its semantic properties. As an illustration, consider the class of inchoative sentences, a class which includes sentences with the abstract inchoative predicate, plus those with such predicates as *become* and *get*, and some with the predicate *go*; for example:

> **6.29**   The whole city went crazy last night.

Many sentences belonging to this class are easy to identify just from examining their surface structures, but others are not. Two which are not are:

> **6.30**   The ice cube melted.
> **6.31** (= **3.22**)   The metal dissolved.

These sentences are easily seen to belong to the class of inchoative sentences, however, when their semantic properties are considered, particularly their paraphrasability by:

> **6.32**   The ice cube became liquid.
> **6.33**   The metal went into solution.

We may even go so far as to say that sentences 6.30 and 6.31 belong to the class of sentences with the abstract inchoative predicate. They differ, however, from those sentences we have considered to belong to that class, for example, 6.23, in that it is not obvious what the predicate is which substitutes for the abstract predicate in them. That is, in 6.23, there is no adjective one can think of in English which when substituted for the abstract inchoative predicate becomes *melt*.[4] What we can do in this situation is to assume that there is an abstract adjective, let us say *melt*,[†] which has the property that it *must* be substituted for the abstract inchoative predicate. We call *melt*[†] an abstract adjective because it is never found to occur as an adjective in English sentences, but only as a substitute for the abstract inchoative predicate. Similarly, on the basis of 6.31 and its paraphrasability by 6.33, we say that there is an abstract adjective *dissolve*[†] which underlies the occurrence of the inchoative predicate *dissolve*.

The opposite situation to this also occurs in English: there are adjectives which cannot replace the abstract inchoative predicate. Among the color adjectives, for example, *green*, *blue*, and *orange* cannot. Thus although we have in English:

6.34   The sky $\begin{Bmatrix} \text{reddened} \\ \text{yellowed} \\ \text{blackened} \end{Bmatrix}$.

we do not have:

6.35   *The sky $\begin{Bmatrix} \text{greened} \\ \text{blued} \\ \text{oranged} \end{Bmatrix}$.

although, of course, we do have:

6.36   The sky became $\begin{Bmatrix} \text{green} \\ \text{blue} \\ \text{orange} \end{Bmatrix}$.

Thus there are, with respect to the abstract inchoative predicate in English, three kinds of adjectives: those like *red*, which can, but do not have to, replace the inchoative predicate; those like *green* which cannot; and those like *melt*,[†] which must.

To complicate matters further, there are inchoative predicates, for example, *wet*, which must in turn be substituted for the abstract causative or instrumental predicate. Thus we have such sentences as:

6.37   The secretary wetted a piece of cotton.

but not:

6.38   *A piece of cotton wetted.

---

[4] Except possibly *molten*, or even more plausibly the past participle *melted*. This observation suggests the possibility of an entirely different syntactic treatment of the inchoative and causative constructions in English, a matter which is taken up in Problem 11 of Chapter 6.
[†] The dagger indicates that the word does not occur as an adjective in English.

This means that the adjective *wet* (among others) can only be substituted for the inchoative predicate provided it is then substituted for the causative or instrumental predicate.[5]

Another typological distinction which can be made on the basis of the rules of 6.1 is that between sentences with a one-place predicate whose argument consists of conjoined noun phrases, and those with a two-place predicate. In Chapter 5 we called the former type symmetric-predicate sentences; the latter may be said to be asymmetric-predicate sentences. In that chapter, we noted that there is a problem in insuring that upon application of the transformation which moves the second conjunct of the subject to a position following the predicate, the correct preposition is put in front of the conjunct. One solution to this problem is simply to associate the preposition with that NP to begin with; in fact, to provide both conjuncts with the same preposition. Thus, we provide sentence 5.126 (repeated here):

6.39 (= 5.126)   The tanker collided with the steamer.

with the deep structure indicated in Fig. 6.14.

There are, however, a few predicates which for various reasons make it difficult for us to classify some sentences containing

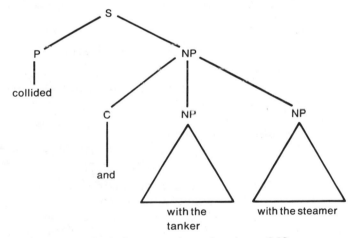

Fig. 6.14. Deep structure of sentence 6.39.

---

[5] The inchoative predicate *wet* may be said to be irregular, in the sense that it obligatorily replaces the causative predicate. Regular inchoative predicates only optionally do so. For discussion of the formal problems associated with matters of regularity and irregularity, see Lakoff (1965). Note that although the verb *wet* can be used intransitively, as in:

(i) The baby just wetted.

Such occurrences are not of the inchoative predicate *wet*, but of the causative predicate with a very special euphemistic meaning. By virtue of this fact, however, we are obliged to consider 6.38 not ungrammatical, but merely internally contradictory.

them. Thus the predicate *kiss* is clearly a symmetric predicate, on the basis of the *E*-grammaticality of:

6.40   Helen and Paris kissed.

and the fact that sentence 6.40 cannot be considered to arise by conjunction reduction from:

6.41   Helen kissed and Paris kissed.

However, the sentences:

6.42   Helen kissed Paris.
6.43   Paris kissed Helen.

do not mean the same thing at all. But this is a problem, since we would expect them to have the same meaning on the basis of *kiss* being a symmetric predicate. One solution to this problem is to say that the transformation which copies the second conjunct of the subject of a symmetric predicate after that predicate is inapplicable to the symmetric predicate *kiss*, and that there is also an asymmetric two-place predicate *kiss* which selects an agent and a locative NP as arguments. Notice that along with example 6.43, the following is perfectly normal:

6.44   Paris kissed Helen's hand.

whereas the sentence:

6.45   Paris' and Helen's hands kissed.

is decidedly internally contradictory (although open to a straightforward metaphoric interpretation). In 6.42 and 6.43, notice also that we interpret the surface-structure objects to be locations (surfaces) as well as persons.

On the other hand, there are a few predicates, such as *sister* and *brother*, which are sometimes symmetric and sometimes asymmetric. Thus we have:

6.46   Sheila and Susan are sisters.
6.47   Sheila is a sister to Susan.

and:

6.48   Susan and Sheila are sisters.
6.49   Susan is a sister to Sheila.

all with the essentially same meaning. But while we have:

6.50   Sheila is a sister to Bruce.

it is contradictory to say:

6.51   Sheila and Bruce are sisters.

Similar observations could be made about the predicate *brother*. What we must say is that if *sister* occurs as a one-place predicate, it requires that its argument be a conjunction of [− Masculine] noun phrases. Notice that then, too, the predicate must appear as a plural noun. On the other hand, if *sister* appears as a two-place predicate, then it imposes no restrictions on the masculinity of its arguments.

Notice also that means must be provided for accounting for such sentences as:

6.52   Sheila and Bruce are brother and sister.

not to mention:

6.53   Sheila and Bruce are husband and wife.

in which the order of conjuncts in the subject does not have to match up with the order of conjuncts in the predicate. It would seem that we require a constituent-structure rule:

6.54   P → C P*

although the only predicates which can be conjoined by means of this rule are those which can substitute for the indefinite pronoun − that is, those which are nouns.[6]

Another dimension along which English sentences can be classified is according to the presence and type of certain kinds of predicates which take sentential noun phrases as arguments. For example, we classify a sentence as a MODAL SENTENCE if the main predicate only tells us something about the truth value, the degree of certainty or possibility, or the necessity of the content of the subordinate clause. The following sentences are therefore modal sentences:

6.55   It is certain that the student knows the answer.
6.56   It is necessary that the student know the answer.
6.57   The student must know the answer.

In all three sentences the predicates *certain, necessary,* and *must* are all one-place predicates which select a sentence as an argument. *Necessary* differs from *certain* in that the main predicate in its subordinate clause is inflected in the so-called subjunctive mood; otherwise we can schematically represent the deep structures of sentences 6.55 and 6.56 as in Fig. 6.15. Sentence 6.57 is in fact ambiguous, and 6.55 and 6.56 can each serve as a paraphrase of one of the possible meanings. That is to say, *must*

---

[6] Rule 6.54 is too powerful as it stands; all that is required is a rule permitting two nouns, which like *brother* and *sister* are antonyms of each other, to be conjoined. The resulting predicate is then symmetric.

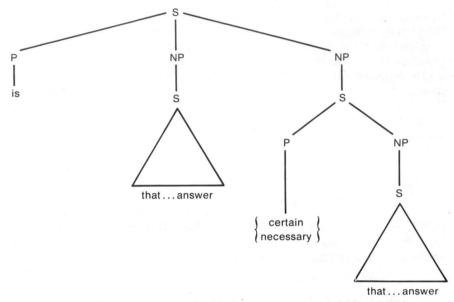

Fig. 6.15. Deep-structure schematization of sentences 6.55 and 6.56.

imposes on its argument either the specification that it is an obligation or that it is a certainty. As we saw in sentence 6.56, obligation is reflected in the subordinate clause by inflecting the verb in the subjunctive mood, but since the argument of *must* is an infinitival clause, the subjunctive mood cannot be expressed in that clause, since infinitives in English do not show the difference between subjunctive and nonsubjunctive moods. The deep structure for sentence 6.57 is given in Fig. 6.16. The surface

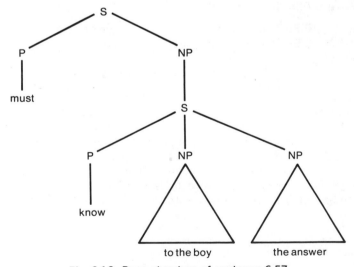

Fig. 6.16. Deep structure of sentence 6.57.

structure for sentence 6.57 is obtained upon application of the subjectivization and infinitive clause separation transformations. The predicate *must*, along with *will, would, shall, should, may, might, can, could*, and *ought*, comprises a class of predicates called the modal predicates, which share a number of quite idiosyncratic syntactic patterns. One is that they are not inflected for so-called present tense (more on this fact below). Thus we do not have:

6.58   *The student musts know the answer.

Another is that their infinitive clause argument cannot have as its main predicate another modal predicate. Thus we do not have:

6.59   *The student must should know the answer.

A third is that, like *must*, they generally impose two different modalities on their argument. Thus, not only is example 6.57 ambiguous, but so are:

6.60   The books may be returned tomorrow.
6.61   Harold should have an answer by tomorrow.
6.62   The pharmacy could be opened tonight.
6.63   The student simply won't do his homework.
6.64   Jesse ought to run a hundred laps today.

Like other predicates which express modality, the English modal predicates give the appearance of being auxiliary to their arguments, and in fact the name given them by both traditional and many generative grammarians is modal auxiliary.

Other predicates which many grammarians have in the past taken as auxiliary constituents in sentences include:

1. the elements which express PERFECT ASPECT, namely the *have* which appears in:

6.65   I have taken a leave of absence for a year.

2. the element which expresses PROGRESSIVE ASPECT, namely the *be* which appears in:

6.66   I'll be going home later.

3. the element which expresses the PASSIVE, namely the *be* appearing in:

6.67   This program may be watched by 25 million people.

And even the element which expresses the TENSE of the verb, the suffix -*ed* italicized in example 6.68, and the suffix -*s* italicized in example 6.69:

6.68   The prisoner tri*ed* to escape yesterday.
6.69   The student know*s* the answer now.

can also be considered independent predicates. It would take far too much space to present the arguments for this position here; let us briefly take up the arguments for the passive and the tense predicates.

Passive sentences such as 6.67 can be considered to constitute a special type of sentence in English; they are usually described as corresponding to so-called active sentences. Thus example 6.67 is said to correspond to the active sentence:

6.70 Twenty-five million people may watch this program.

In order for an active sentence to have a passive counterpart, its main predicate must be at least a two-place one, and one of the arguments must be an agent or instrumental NP. In the passive counterpart, the predicate corresponding to the main predicate of the active sentence occurs as a so-called past participle (*watched* is the past participle of *watch*, for example), which is in fact an adjective. Thus the deep structure of sentence 6.67 is as in Fig. 6.17. The deep structure of sentence 6.70 is, on

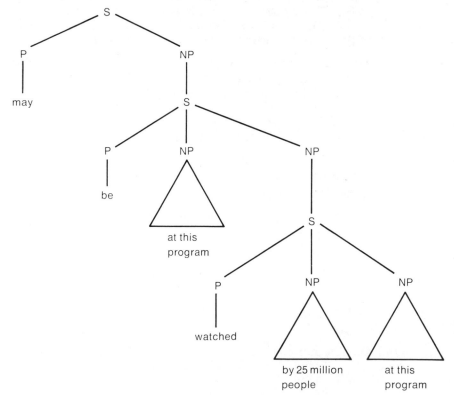

Fig. 6.17. Deep structure of sentence 6.67.

the other hand, as given in Fig. 6.18. By comparing Figs. 6.17 and 6.18 the reader can easily see for himself that the passive predicate occurs with all the arguments with which its active counterpart occurs; the difference is that the passive predicate must occur in a sentential argument of *be*.

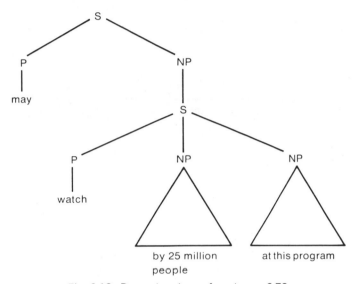

Fig. 6.18. Deep structure of sentence 6.70.

There is one other difference, too, namely that the passive predicate is always permitted to occur without the agent argument, as in the sentence:

6.71 This program may be watched.

which has the deep structure illustrated in Fig. 6.19. Passive predicates without agent arguments are generally felt to express states rather than activities; this is especially clear when we compare such sentences as:

6.72 The little girl was hurt by the bully.
6.73 The little girl was hurt.

Passive predicates may be considered adjectival forms of predicates that select agent arguments; predicates which select dative arguments, on the other hand, have another corresponding adjectival predicate, one which generally, but not always, is characterized by the so-called present-participial suffix *-ing*. Re-

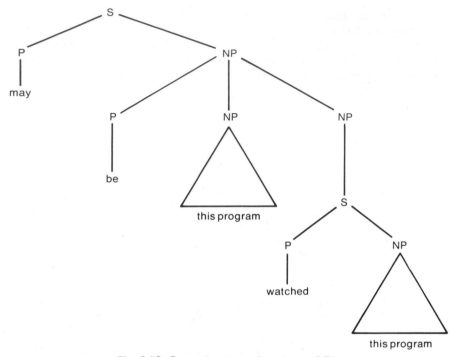

Fig. 6.19. Deep structure of sentence 6.71.

call, for example, sentences 3.32 and 3.33, which we repeat:

> **6.74 (= 3.32)** Strangers frightened our little chihuahua.
>
> **6.75 (= 3.33)** Strangers were frightening to our little chihuahua.

Sentence 6.74 is ambiguous, whereas 6.75 is not, a fact which was noted in Chapter 3. Under one interpretation of 6.74, *strangers* is an agent NP, in which case the sentence has the passive counterpart:

> **6.76** Our little chihuahua was frightened by strangers.

Under the other, *strangers* is not an agent NP, and *our little chihuahua* is a dative NP, and it is this sense of *frighten* which has the adjectival counterpart *frightening*. Going a little more deeply into sentence 6.74 we note that under the first interpretation of it, *frighten* is the causative of an inchoative predicate, while under the other interpretation it is simply an inchoative predicate (the underlying adjective is, of course, *afraid*). The first sense of sentence 6.74 is paraphrasable as:

6.77   Strangers caused our little chihuahua to become afraid.

while the second is paraphrasable as:

6.78   Our little chihuahua became afraid at the sight of strangers.

The claim that the tense of the verb is actually itself a predicate is difficult to establish convincingly; our approach here will be to assume it and consider some of the consequences of the assumption. We say first of all that the tense predicate is an abstract predicate which occurs in every sentence type. Next we say that it is a two-place predicate; one argument is a time expression, the other is a sentence. Thus the deep structure for sentences 6.68 and 6.69 is as in Figs. 6.20 and 6.21. The abstract

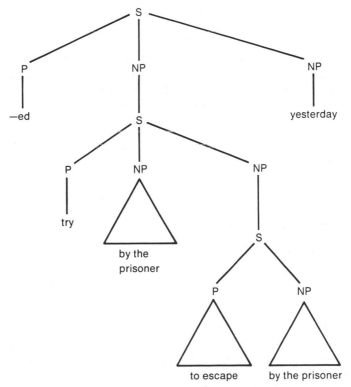

Fig. 6.20. Deep structure of sentence 6.68.

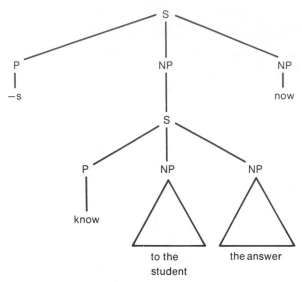

Fig. 6.21. Deep structure of sentence 6.69.

tense predicates have been spelled with their characteristic suffix in these figures. To obtain the surface structures of these sentences from these deep structures, the usual rules are applied. By considering the tense constituent to be a predicate, we provide a natural way of accounting for the relationship between the choice of so-called time adverbs and the tense of the verb. The past-tense predicate requires that its time argument specify past time; if it does not, an internal contradiction arises. Similarly the present-time predicate requires its time expression to specify nonpast time. Many other syntactic phenomena, for example the so-called sequence of tense patternings, are easily describable within the framework of considering tense to be a predicate.

Three sentence types remain to be discussed in this chapter; along one dimension we will consider IMPERATIVE and INTERROGATIVE sentence types, and along another, NEGATIVE sentence types. We have already pointed out, in Chapters 2 and 5, that in the deep structure of an imperative sentence there appears an argument which is transformationally deleted, one which has the referential index or indices of the pronoun *you*. Moreover, an imperative sentence such as 2.37 (repeated here):

6.79 (= **2.37**) Take these clothes to the laundry.

has approximately the same meaning as:

6.80 I order you to take these clothes to the laundry.

This observation suggests that in the deep structure underlying imperative sentences there is an abstract imperative predicate which has the same selectional features as verbs like *order*, *command*, and *request*. The deep structure for sentence 6.79 would then be as in Fig. 6.22. The abstract imperative predicate

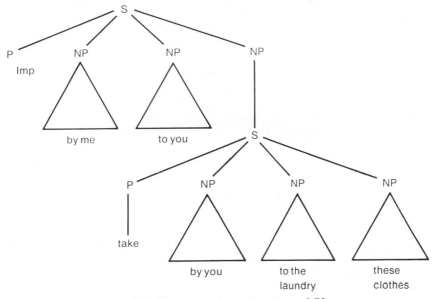

Fig. 6.22. Deep structure of sentence 6.79.

is a three-place predicate, two of whose arguments are fixed. The agent is expressed always by the first-person pronoun, and the dative by the second-person pronoun (or an NP coreferential with it). The third argument is the content of the command, and in it the second-person pronoun must occur as an agent. This requirement accounts for the fact that a sentence such as:

6.81   Know the answer to the question.

is difficult to construe as an imperative, since *you* occurs only as a dative argument to *know*, not as an agent argument.[7] To obtain the surface structure of sentence 6.79 from its deep structure, the usual rules of subjectivization, infinitival-clause separation, and reflexive pronoun deletion apply; moreover the agent and dative arguments of the abstract predicate are deleted, and of course the predicate *take* is substituted for the abstract predi-

---

[7] The most natural interpretation of 6.81 is as an expression of a condition; in a discourse it could for example plausibly occur after a rhetorical question such as:

(i)   Would you like a free trip for two to Bermuda?

See Problem 4 of Chapter 2 for other examples of this type.

cate. The dative argument of the imperative predicate need not be deleted, and in fact is not deleted if it is not the pronoun *you*, as in:

6.82 Everybody duck!

The abstract imperative predicate can also be considered to be one of the modal predicates, despite the fact that it is a three-place one, inasmuch as the other modal predicates do not occur with it in English sentences.

By a similar argument, it can be maintained that in the deep structure of interrogative sentences such as:

6.83 Are you taking these clothes to the laundry?

there is an abstract interrogative predicate corresponding to the overt predicate *ask* in the sentence:

6.84 I ask whether you are taking these clothes to the laundry.

The abstract interrogative predicate has two arguments, one which is fixed as the first-person agent and the other which is a sentence. The sentential argument of the abstract interrogative predicate moreover is to be considered a disjunction, that is, two sentences connected by the disjunctive conjunction *or*. Sentence 6.82 is to be viewed as having been reduced by the conjunction-reduction transformation from:

6.85 Are you taking these clothes to the laundry or aren't you taking these clothes to the laundry?

Other possible consequences of the conjunction-reduction transformation to the structure underlying 6.85 are:

6.86 Are you taking these clothes to the laundry or aren't you?

6.87 Are you taking these clothes to the laundry or not?

Similarly, the conjunction-reduction transformation has applied to the structure underlying 6.84; another possible application of this transformation to that structure results in:

6.88 I ask whether you are taking these clothes to the laundry or not.

Each disjunct in the deep structure of an interrogative sentence is a potential answer to the question being asked. Thus the semantic interpretation of 6.83 is roughly that it is a request for someone to specify which of the disjuncts is the answer to it. Since a reply such as *yes* or *no* uniquely specifies which one is the answer, such replies count as acceptable answers to the question. On the other hand, replies such as silence, *maybe, who knows?* count as evasions of the question, while replies such as *there's a fly on your nose* would count as irrelevant to the question.

Interrogative sentences which are introduced by one of the question words *who, what, which, whose, where, when, why*, and *how* are similar in deep structure to questions such as 6.83, which are not introduced by such words. For example, the question:

6.89 Who saw the *Today* show yesterday?

can be considered to be essentially equivalent in meaning to:

6.90 I ask who saw the *Today* show yesterday.

Moreover, sentence 6.89 represents a transformationally reduced disjunction of potential answers; but in this case the disjunction has been reduced to the disjunction of referential indices associated with the question word *who*. The fact that *who* stands for a disjunction of persons accounts for the seemingly puzzling fact that the word itself is singular; for example, we have:

6.91 Who is coming?

and not (in Standard American English at least):

6.92 *Who are coming?

yet the answer may be plural:

6.93 Tom, Dick, and Harry are coming.

Two special transformations apply to sentences containing the abstract interrogative pronoun. One is that the question word — more precisely, the NP containing the question word — is moved to the front of the entire sentence; the other is that if any modal predicate, the predicate *be*, or the predicate *have* is present, then the first of these is moved to a position immediately following the question word, or if there is none, to the front of the sentence. In case there is no such predicate present, then the predicate *do*, together with the tense predicate, is so moved. These observations account for the form of such questions as:

6.94 What will you see in New York?
6.95 What could you be seeing in New York?
6.96 What are you seeing in New York?
6.97 Are you seeing anyone in New York?

6.98 What does one see in New York?
6.99 Does one see anything in New York?

corresponding to:

6.100 I ask what you will see in New York.
6.101 I ask what you could be seeing in New York.
6.102 I ask what you are seeing in New York.
6.103 I ask whether you are seeing anyone in New York.
6.104 I ask what one sees in New York.
6.105 I ask whether one sees anything in New York.

The exact form that these transformations should take has been the subject of much discussion in the literature. For early

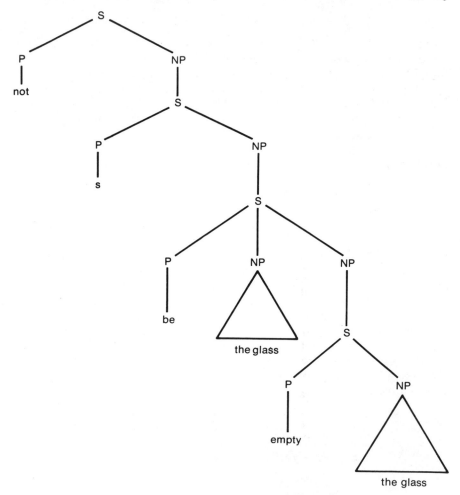

Fig. 6.23. Deep structure of sentence 6.106.

formulations, see Chomsky (1957) and Lees (1960). For a somewhat later formulation, see Katz and Postal (1964). For a formulation of corresponding rules in French, see Langacker (1965).

A satisfactory treatment of the structure of negative sentences is not possible here. For a sampling of just some of the
problems involved in producing a satisfactory treatment, see
Klima (1964) and Fillmore (1967). The simplest kind of negative
sentence is one which contains the constituent *not*; for example:

6.106   The glass is not empty.

In such sentences the negative constituent has certain of the
characteristics of a one-place predicate. It can occur only once
(this is the familiar dictum about multiple negation), and its
semantic domain is the entire remainder of the sentence. Thus,
we are led to postulate the deep structure for sentence 6.106
shown in Fig. 6.23 (we include the tense predicate). The problem
is that the sense of negation can also attach itself to other constituents, either OVERTLY, as with the negative indefinite pronouns *no one, nothing, never, nowhere,* and the negative predicates
unhappy, disconnected; or COVERTLY, as with the negative predicates *doubt, deny, wrong,* or in such expressions as *hardly,
scarcely, barely, few.* Problems related to this property of the
negative predicate in English are taken up by both Klima and
Fillmore in the references mentioned above.

7 MORPHOLOGY

In this chapter we deal with the way in which the categories and feature specifications underlying the sentences of a natural language are realized as elements which ultimately are to be spoken or written. We can think of the rules governing the construction of deep structures as providing categories (S, P, IP, NP, C) and feature specifications which are in turn operated on in various ways by the transformational rules. It is important to realize that no transformational rule need make reference to the way in which the constituents of a structure are to be spoken or written, but only to the categories and features present in the structure. This means that we do not need rules of the form 3.3 in the constituent-structure component of the grammar, but only rules of the form 3.2 (that is, rules 6.1 and 6.53), plus rules which insert bundles of feature specifications for each of the categories P, IP, and C. The rules which specify how a sentence is to be spoken or written may be applied after all the transformational rules have been applied.

We are concerned here only with the most general rules which make such a specification, not with the rules which are concerned with the minute details of pronunciation or orthography. We use the traditional linguistic term MORPHOLOGY as the label for this kind of study because we are after the rules which govern the general form of the speaking and writing of sentences.

The simplest situation is presented by having a category together with its bundle of specifications correspond to a minimally significant unit, or MORPHEME, which itself is expressed in a string of elements of pronunciation known as PHONEMES, each of which in writing generally corresponds to a single letter of the alphabet. The phonemes are themselves analyzable as bundles of feature specifications, in which the features have to do with the activities of the mechanism of speech, notably the vocal cords, the tongue, and the lips. The phonemes which express morphemes can be thought of as being strung together by very general rules governing the phonemic structure of morphemes. If a morpheme or sequence can be uttered in isolation by linguistically untrained fluent speakers as an element of their language, we call it also a WORD. Morphemes which, on the one hand, correspond to a single category and its bundle of features and which, on the other, are words in English include such things as *boy, word, go, Mississippi, one, and.* Clearly, however there are morphemes which are not words—for example, those corresponding to the tense predicate; and there are single bundles of features which are realized by strings of morphemes, for example, *blackbird, tigress, undergo, inside;* and even strings of words, for example *take place, go by, billy goat.*

One of the most interesting problems of morphology is the analysis of what goes on when a particular bundle of features associated with some predicate is moved into the position of an abstract predicate. One of several things can happen. Let us assume for simplicity of discussion that the particular bundle of features, when it is not substituted for the abstract predicate, is realized by a morpheme which is also a word. First, the bundle of features may retain its morphological identity, the abstract predicate having no morphological realization. Thus when the features realized by *yellow, level, warm* are substituted for the inchoative predicate, the morphological realization remains *yellow, level,* and *warm.* Second, the morpheme may retain its identity, the abstract predicate being realized as a prefix or suffix to this morpheme. Thus, when the features underlying *red, thick, rough* are substituted for the inchoative predicate, the results are *redden, thicken, roughen.* The suffix *-en* is the realization of the features underlying the abstract inchoative predicate. When predicates *walk, rob, bat* are substituted for the past-tense predicate we get *walked, robbed, batted,* in which the suffix *-ed* expresses the past-tense predicate. Third, the morpheme may undergo some internal modification of its phonological makeup while the abstract predicate has no realization. The result is a single morpheme, but a different one from that which has not undergone the substitution. Thus, when *run, give, fly, send, bite, stand* are substituted for the past-tense predicate, the resulting morphemes are *ran, gave, flew, sent, bit, stood.* Fourth, the morpheme may undergo some internal modification, the abstract predicate being also realized as a prefix or suffix. Thus when *sleep, leave, mean, teach, think, make* are substituted for the past-tense predicate, we get *slept, left, meant* (a vowel change occurs that is unreflected in the spelling), *taught, thought, made.*

Similarly the inchoative counterparts to *long* and *strong* are *lengthen* and *strengthen*. Fifth, a morpheme may appear which bears no phonological relationship to the original morpheme (that is, which is SUPPLETIVE). Thus the past-tense forms of *go, be* are *went, was* (also *were*). Sixth, a suppletive morpheme may appear together with a suffix or prefix which is the realization of the abstract predicate. An instance of this may be seen in the inchoative form of *afraid*, namely *frighten*. Still other possibilities exist, but this inventory contains most of them.

At this point we may make a distinction which is well known in linguistics, that between INFLECTION and DERIVATION. The main distinguishing characteristic which separates verbs from adjectives and nouns is that verbs must be substituted for an abstract predicate, whereas adjectives and nouns do not have to be. Verbs must be substituted for either the abstract tense predicate or the abstract infinitival predicate. In Chapter 6 we did not indicate the need for an abstract infinitival predicate, but it can be shown to play the same role in infinitival clauses that the abstract tense predicate plays in main and subordinate relative and *that*-clauses. It is a one- or two-place predicate, one of whose arguments is a time-NP (this argument is dispensable) and the other a sentential one. Thus we represent the deep structure of the ambiguous sentence (ambiguous in written form; in speech the two interpretations differ):

7.1 Willie wants to leave now.

as in Figs. 7.1 and 7.2.

Since a verb must be substituted for one or the other of these abstract predicates, it will always appear in either a tense form or an infinitival form.[1] These are called the inflected forms of the verb; the totality of inflected forms that a verb can take is traditionally called its CONJUGATION. The infinitival form of the verb in English is very easy to describe morphologically; it consists of the regular morphological form of the verb and (optionally) the separable prefix *to* (which is, moreover, written as a separate word). Whether or not the prefix appears depends on the predicate of the clause containing the infinitival clause. If it is an abstract predicate, one of the modal predicates other than *ought* or one of the verbs *let, make, have, see, hear, feel,* and a few others, then the prefix is missing; otherwise it is present.[2]

---

[1] The verb may also appear in a so-called gerund form, which is morphologically characterized by the suffix *-ing*, as in the sentence:

(i) John started taking oboe lessons last Thursday.

[2] In many reference grammars of English, the infinitive without *to* is called the "unmarked infinitive," on the grounds that no particular morpheme marks or indicates its presence. According to our use of the terms "marked" and "unmarked," however, it is the infinitive

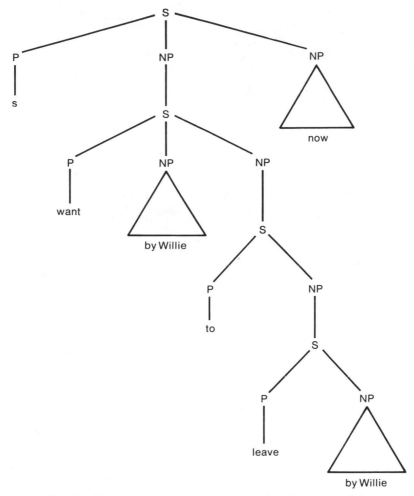

Fig. 7.1. Deep structure of one interpretation of sentence 7.1.

On the other hand, the past-tense conjugation of English verbs is quite complicated morphologically, as we have seen above. The vast majority of verbs form their past tense with the suffix spelled *-(e)d*, and undergo no internal change. These are the so-called WEAK VERBS, sometimes referred to, rather misleadingly, as the verbs with a regular past-tense form. The hundred or so

with *to* which is the unmarked one. In standard English, *ought* occurs without *to* in questions and negative sentences, while *make, see, hear,* and *feel* occur with *to* in passive sentences, as for example in:

(i)   The patient was made to wait for an hour.

With the verbs *dare* and *need* matters are somewhat more complex; see Problem 7 of Chapter 7.

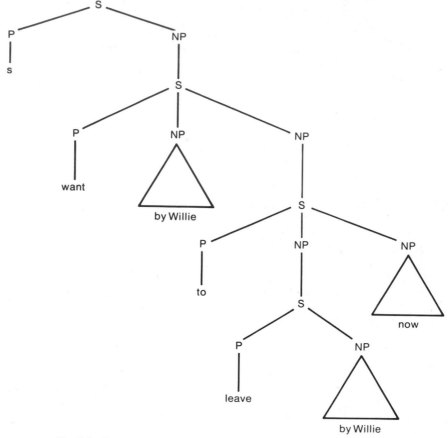

Fig. 7.2. Deep structure of another interpretation of sentence 7.1.

verbs with so-called irregular past-tense forms, namely those which undergo internal vowel changes and which occur either with no suffix at all or a suffix spelled -*t*, actually can be described by means of rules; it is simply that these morphological rules are by and large special to these forms.

The present-tense forms of the verb turn out to depend upon the number of the noun phrase which has been made its subject and also upon whether or not the subject is a first- or second-person pronoun. Traditionally, the present-tense form is said to agree in person and number with its subject NP. If the subject is singular in number and is not a first- or second-person pronoun, then the present-tense predicate is realized as the suffix spelled -*(e)s* which is attached to the verb.[3] Otherwise, no suffix is at-

---

[3] The verbs *have, do, say* also undergo slight internal modification upon addition of the present-tense suffix.

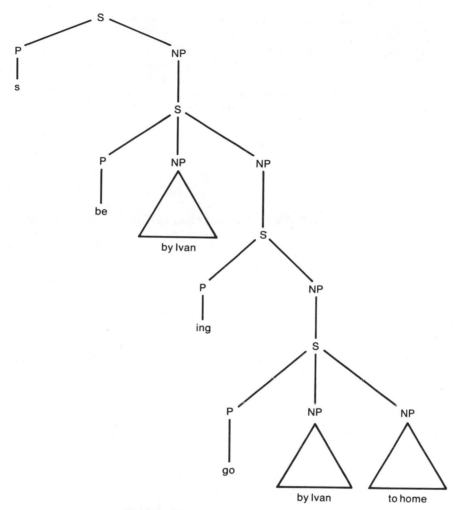

Fig. 7.3. Deep structure of sentence 7.2.

tached. The one exception to these observations is provided by the verb *be*, which takes on the suppletive forms *am*, *are*, or *is*, depending upon the person and number of the subject. The form is *am* if the subject is the first-person singular pronoun *I*, *is* if it is singular and not first or second person, and *are* otherwise.[4]

In addition to the infinitival and tense forms of the verb, the

---

[4]These forms also occur contracted, by loss of their initial vowel. The contracted form of *is* (and also *has)* is then subject to the same rules of pronunciation as affect the plural, possessive, and third person singular present tense suffixes. Curiously, therefore, no phonetic distinction is made between the contracted and uncontracted forms of *is* and *has* when they occur following such words as *Ross*, *Rose*, *church*, and *judge*.

so-called present- and past-participle forms are also usually included among the inflectional forms of the verb. The present participle, which is formed with the suffix -*ing* (it is thus identical in form with the gerund; see footnote 1) is said to indicate progressive aspect, which we can also consider to be an abstract predicate in English (a fact noted very briefly in Chapter 6). Thus we would set up the deep structure indicated in Fig. 7.3 for sentence 7.2:

7.2 Ivan is going home.

The past participle of the English verb, which like the past-tense form has a quite complex morphological description, is used either to indicate perfect aspect of the verb or passive voice. On the basis of our discussion in this chapter, it would seem preferable to analyze the deep structure of passive sentences in a slightly different way from our treatment in Chapter 6. In particular, the deep structure of sentence 6.67 (repeated below) instead of being as indicated in Fig. 6.17, is as indicated in Fig. 7.4.

7.3 (= 6.67) This program may be watched by 25 million people.

Morphologically, the past participle is formed in the following ways. The vast majority of verbs undergo no internal change and the suffix spelled -*(e)d* is attached; thus for most verbs the past-participle form is identical with the past-tense form. Similarly, most verbs which form their past tense with -*t* and an internal vowel change form their past participle identically. A considerable number of those verbs which form their past tense by means of internal vowel modification alone or by suppletion, form their past participle by means of a suffix variously spelled, -*n*, -*en*, and -*ne*. They may also undergo internal vowel modification. Thus *take, eat, fly, hide, go, be* have the past participles *taken, eaten, flown, hidden, gone, been.* A few undergo internal vowel modification alone; for example *drink, find* have the past participles *drunk, found.* Finally a few undergo no change at all; thus *run, put*, have the past participles *run, put* (the latter verb also undergoes no change in the past tense).

According to the way in which we are drawing the inflection versus derivation distinction, the formation of the present and past participles counts as derivation; the resultant forms are in fact adjectives. These are very general derivational processes, however, since every verb has a corresponding present- and past-participle form. A much more restricted derivational formation is the formation of inchoative verbs from adjectives. We have

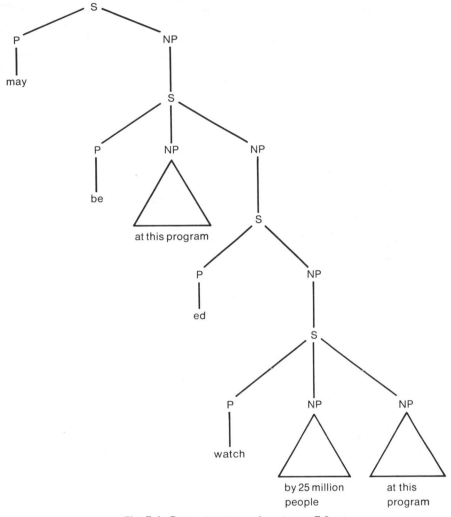

Fig. 7.4. Deep structure of sentence 7.3.

already noted that there are many adjectives which do not replace the abstract inchoative predicate. Those that do so behave
morphologically in one of the following ways. They may undergo
no change at all—for example, *dirty, yellow, warm, cool, wet;*
they may undergo no change, the inchoative predicate being
realized as the suffix *-en*—for example, *ripe, hard, soft, rough,
thick, smooth, loose;* one or two undergo internal change—for
example, the inchoative of *hot* is *heat.* A few take the prefix

en-; thus the inchoatives of *rich, large* are *enrich, enlarge.*[5] There are those which do not occur as adjectives at all in surface structures, for example, *melt*[†] and *rise.*[†] Finally, we have noted some whose inchoative forms must substitute for the abstract causative or instrumental predicate; among those listed above are *dirty, wet,* and *rich.*

It will be noted that those adjectives which form their inchoative counterparts with *-en* are all monosyllabic morphemes ending in a stop (for example, *d, t, k*) or fricative (for example, *f, th, s*). This observation is typical of many which could be made about morphology; the particular formations which are found may be governed by rules which take into account the phonological properties of morphemes.

Other derivational formations of considerable interest are those of nouns from verbs and adjectives, and vice versa. Thus given a noun such as *joy,* we can form the adjectives *joyous* and *joyful,* and from these the nouns *joyousness* and *joyfulness.* One of the most difficult problems related to such patterns is to determine whether in fact there is derivational formation (substitution of a predicate for an abstract predicate), or simply some sort of lexical relationship. Consider for example the relationship between the verb *address* and the noun *address;* in particular consider this noun in each of the following sentences:

> **7.4** The President's address last night to Congress inspired the nation.
> **7.5** The President's address is 1600 Pennsylvania Avenue.

In sentence 7.4, the noun *address* would seem to be best considered to be derived from the verb *address* meaning *speak before.* Thus we set up the deep structure of sentence 7.4 as in Fig. 7.5, in which P_{Nom} represents the abstract nominalization predicate. In sentence 7.5, however, there would seem to be no point in analyzing *address* as the nominalization of the verb *address* meaning *designate for;* rather, we would say that the relationship between them is that they are separate lexical items

---

[5] There are some very special inchoative forms, also. Some which we have already noted are *frighten, lengthen,* and *strengthen,* based on the adjectives *afraid, long,* and *strong* respectively. *Enliven* and *embolden* appear to be formed by both prefixation and suffixation from *alive* and *bold. Worsen* is presumably the inchoative of *bad,* but *better* is certainly not the inchoative of *good* (this adjective has no morphological inchoative, although *improve* comes close semantically). A puzzling fact about *worsen,* in my speech at least, is that it is not used in causative sentences with agentive subjects, although it can be with instrumental ones. Thus I make the following grammaticality judgments:

(i) *The doctor worsened his patient's condition by giving him an overdose of sedative.

(ii) An overdose of sedative worsened the patient's condition.

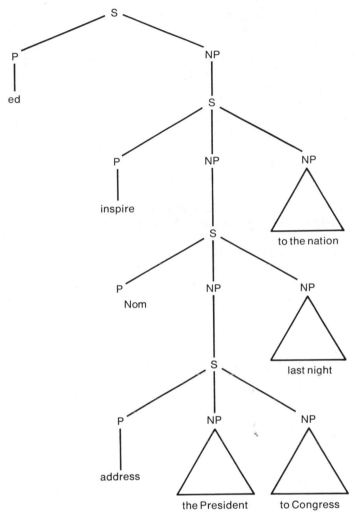

Fig. 7.5. Deep structure of sentence 7.4.

which share certain semantic features and also happen to have very similar morphological realizations.[6]

Let us now look briefly at noun morphology. One problem

---

[6]This position can be extended to cover all cases of nominalization, including the one illustrated in 7.4, and indeed all items related by derivational morphology. Thus one could hold that, for example, the causative verb *heat* is simply a lexical item which shares some features with the adjective *hot*, but that the surface structures of sentences containing it are not arrived at transformationally from deep structures containing embedded sentences whose predicates are *hot* and the abstract inchoative predicate. This position is advanced in Chomsky (forthcoming). For further consideration of this matter see Problem 11 of Chapter 6. For Chomsky's earlier thinking on this question, see Chomsky (1965, section 4.3, pp. 184-192).

that we noted in Chapter 4 is of interest here: certain feature specifications, for example [-Masculine], may be associated with particular nouns, suffixes, as in *tigress*. We can regard *tigress* as syntactically a simple predicate, quite on a par with *tiger*, but for it to be realized morphologically, the specification [-Masculine] must separate off, as it were, and become associated with a suffixal morpheme.

A more serious problem that has concerned us all along in this book has been the formation of plural nouns, which we have said arise from the conjunction of nouns identical except for their referential indices. The morphological realization of plural nouns can be described in a relatively straightforward way. The vast majority of them form the plural by the addition of the suffix spelled *-(e)s*, but a few indicate it rather by an internal vowel change; for example, the plural forms of *man, tooth, mouse, foot*, are *men, teeth, mice, feet*. In these cases, we would not want to say that the plural forms consist of two morphemes, but rather that the indication of plurality has not been separated off from the other features of the nouns in question.

Certain nouns, for example *scissors* and *pants*, have the curious property of being plural in form but not necessarily so in meaning. Thus, despite the apparent plurality of *pants*, it is a contradiction to say:

7.6   The pants I'm wearing look alike.

To indicate the semantic plurality of these predicates unambiguously, one may quantify them by means of the expression *pairs of*.

This observation relates to another problem regarding plural formation—that there are many nouns in English which generally are not conjoined with different referential indices. These are the so-called mass nouns, such as *milk, rice, blood*. However, such nouns, like many others, can be quantified; which is to say that one can construct noun phrases like *a bottle of milk, a pile of rice, a pint of blood*, and the like, by means of rather complex transformational rules operating on relative-clause structures something like *milk which is in a bottle*, and so forth. These expressions, then, can be conjoined with different referential indices, resulting in plural noun phrases such as *bottles of milk*.[7]

---

[7] Under certain circumstances, however, mass nouns can occur in the plural. Thus, although *coffee* is a mass noun, we can speak of *the coffees of South America, a blend of five different coffees*, and the like. But such occurrences are always equivalent to, and can be considered transformationally reduced forms of, expressions like *kinds of coffee*. Notice that similar expressions containing ordinary count nouns like *coin* can undergo the same reduction, so that the expression *the coins of England* can refer either to the collection of all English coins or to the various kinds of English coins, for example, the ha'penny, penny, and so forth.

The expression *a bottle of milk* can, however, arise from a different deep structure. The noun *bottle* can be considered to be a one-place predicate which selects as arguments noun phrases like *of milk* (anything which can go into bottles). As a result we can say both:

7.7 I just drank a bottle of milk.

and:

7.8 I just broke a bottle of milk.

In 7.7, clearly, *milk* is the head noun of the NP *a bottle of milk*, while in 7.8, *bottle* is the head noun of the NP.

We have left for the end of this chapter perhaps the most difficult of all problems of noun morphology, that of the definite and indefinite articles *the, a, an*. The difficulty lies in determining how they arise in surface structures. If an N is referentially fixed, then it will obligatorily occur with the definite article or without any article at all. The former case is exemplified by *The Bronx, The Hague*, and *The University of Chicago;* the latter by *Manhattan, Rotterdam*, and *Harvard University*.[8] If an N is not referentially fixed, then in a discourse its reference will be fixed at some point by means of its use in some sentence, or by assumption on the part of the participants that the reference is known. The definite article then arises in the following way: it is the reduction of a relative clause meaning *whose reference has been fixed*. The indefinite article, on the other hand, is often the reduction of a relative clause meaning *whose reference is hereby fixed*. This formulation accounts for the fact that generally an NP appears in a discourse with a particular reference only once with the indefinite article. Its subsequent appearances are always with the definite article. For further discussion concerning the articles in English, see Smith (1964) and Bach (1968), and for an illuminating philosophical analysis, see Russell (1916).

---

[8] This is not to say that such nouns cannot occur without articles, but that if they do, they are not terms with fixed reference. Indeed, in the following sentence, *Manhattan Island* makes no reference at all:

(i) You can't buy a Manhattan Island for $24 anymore.

8 WHY DEEP AND SURFACE STRUCTURE?

The deep structure of a sentence is a representation of the meaning of that sentence; however; it is not deep structures which are spoken and written by people, but rather surface structures. Despite this, fluent speakers have no difficulty in saying what they mean, nor do they have trouble in understanding what other people say to them. The reason difficulty is not generally encountered is that surface structures provide access to deep structures; alternatively, we say that deep structures are ACCESSIBLE from surface structures. Just how it is that fluent speakers obtain the deep structures of the sentences they hear, or how they form surface structures to say or write, given the meaning of their intentions, is not understood. In all likelihood they do *not* use the rules of grammar themselves, but rather a set of processes which are based on those rules.

There are, however, surface structures which, because of their complexity, do not permit ready access to their deep structures. As an experiment, read example 8.1 below to a fluent speaker of English who has not heard it before, or alternatively, read it to yourself aloud quickly, and without glancing back.

> **8.1** The rumor that that the report which the advisory committee submitted was supressed is true is preposterous.

In all likelihood you will find that the hearer will not comprehend example 8.1 at all even though it is a perfectly *E*-grammatical linguistic object. Next, try the same experiment with examples 8.2 through 8.5.

8.2 The rumor that it is true that the report which the advisory committee submitted was suppressed is preposterous.

8.3 The rumor is preposterous that it is true that the report which the advisory committee submitted was suppressed.

8.4 The rumor that it is true that the report was suppressed which the advisory committee submitted is preposterous.

8.5 The rumor is preposterous that it is true that the report was suppressed which the advisory committee submitted.

These examples you will likely find comprehensible to fluent English speakers, although you may find examples 8.3 through 8.5 more readily comprehensible than 8.2. If you examine sentences 8.1–8.5 carefully, you will discover that they all have the same deep structure. Their surface structures differ only in that the extraposition transformation has not been applied at all to sentence 8.1; that it has been applied once (to the clause *that the report . . . suppressed*) to 8.2; twice (to the clauses *that the report . . . suppressed* and *that it is true . . . suppressed*) to 8.3; twice (to the clauses *that the report . . . suppressed* and *which . . . submitted*) to 8.4; and three times (to the clauses *that the report . . . suppressed, that it is true . . . suppressed,* and *which . . . submitted*) to 8.5.

The reason sentence 8.1 is incomprehensible is that the clauses which constitute it are buried inside one another. The clause *which . . . submitted* is completely enclosed within the clause *the report . . . was suppressed,* which in turn is completely enclosed within the clause *that the report . . . is true,* which finally is completely enclosed within the main clause *the rumor . . . is preposterous.* A clause which is completely enclosed within another is said to be SELF-EMBEDDED; if a clause, such as *which . . . submitted* in sentence 8.1, is self-embedded three times, then the sentence as a whole is practically incomprehensible (Chomsky 1965, section 1.2; Miller and Isard 1964). In sentence 8.2, the most deeply self-embedded clause is also *which . . . submitted,* but in that sentence it is self-embedded only twice. In examples 8.3 and 8.4 no clause is self-embedded more than once, while in 8.5 there are no self-embedded clauses. Sentences are generally comprehensible when they do not contain clauses which are self-embedded three or more times, and the less self-embedding there is in a sentence, the more readily comprehensible such a sentence is.

The results of the foregoing "experiment" show that in order to produce comprehensibly the deep structure underlying sentences 8.1–8.5, the extraposition transformation must be applied at least once; put another way, if there were no extraposition transformation in English, there would be no means of producing a surface structure which would provide ready access to that deep structure. This observation amounts to an explanation of the existence of the extraposition transformation in English on the basis of the need to render certain otherwise inaccessible deep structures accessible.

On the other hand, there are deep structures which are rendered incomprehensible if the extraposition transformation *is* applied. To see this, consider the sentence:

> **8.6** That Tom's told everyone that he's staying proves that it's true that he's thinking that it would be a good idea for him to show that he likes it here.

Sentence 8.6, as it stands, is comprehensible to fluent English speakers, but if the extraposition transformation is applied to the *that*-clause subject of the verb *proves*, the resulting sentence, while still *E*-grammatical, is relatively incomprehensible.

> **8.7** It proves that it's true that Tom's thinking that it would be a good idea for him to show that he likes it here that he's told everyone that he's staying.

The reason sentence 8.7 is relatively less comprehensible than 8.6 is that certain clauses which are not self-embedded in 8.6 (for example the clause *that it's true . . . here*) are self-embedded in 8.7. Thus, while the extraposition transformation has the effect in certain cases of reducing self-embedding, in other cases it has the effect of increasing it. We would expect that when the application of the extraposition transformation would increase the amount of self-embedding, the rule would be optional. This is indeed what we find, as we have seen in Chapter 5. Thus the optionality of transformations can be explained, at least in part, on the basis of the need to preserve the grammaticality of the surface structures which alone provide access to certain deep structures, for example the deep structure underlying sentences 8.6 and 8.7.[1]

From these considerations, and from what we have shown in Chapters 5–7, we conclude that the meaning of a sentence is represented in terms of a structure provided by constituent-structure rules having the form of rules of symbolic logic. This structure, which is called the deep structure of that sentence, is transformed by syntactic rules into a structure which is ulti-

---

[1] For further discussion of these matters, see Langendoen (forthcoming a).

mately spoken or written, called its surface structure. These rules are such that given a deep structure, there is a surface structure which provides access to that deep structure. There is nothing meaningful that cannot be comprehended.

Present-day generative-transformational research on the structure of language is proceeding along several fronts. First of all, a considerable amount of work is being done on the problem of exactly specifying the nature of deep structures. The formulation given in this book is undoubtedly wrong in numerous details and perhaps also in certain fundamental respects. Secondly, the study of the nature of the lexicon, and of the problem of providing a representation for the semantic content of lexical items, is being pursued. Many fundamental questions are still unanswered, for example the question of the exact representation of the meaning of items such as *melt* in English. The suggestion that there is a lexical item *melt*[t] which obligatorily undergoes substitution for the abstract inchoative predicate (our suggestion in Chapters 6 and 7) may or may not be the most satisfactory one. Certainly other "solutions" to the problem are possible, as we have in fact suggested at various points. Third, research on transformational rules is being intensively pursued; however, the examination of transformational rules in light of their role in providing access to deep structures is only beginning now.

BIBLIOGRAPHY

Austin, J. L.: *How to Do Things with Words*. Cambridge: Harvard University Press, 1962.

Bach, Emmon: Nouns and Noun-Phrases. In: Bach and Harms (Eds.): *Universals in Linguistic Theory*. New York: Holt, Rinehart and Winston, 1968.

Bach, Emmon, and Robert Harms (Eds.): *Universals in Linguistic Theory*. New York: Holt, Rinehart and Winston, 1968.

Bendix, Edward H.: *Componential Analysis of General Vocabulary: The Semantic Structure of a Set of Verbs in English, Hindi, and Japanese* (Publication 41 of the Research Center in Anthropology, Folklore, and Linguistics). Bloomington and The Hague: Indiana University Press and Mouton and Company, 1966.

Bever, Thomas G., and Weksel, William (Eds.): *The Structure and Psychology of Language*. New York: Holt, Rinehart and Winston, forthcoming.

Bierwisch, Manfred: Some Semantic Universals of German Adjectivals. In: *Foundations of Language* 3, 1967, pp. 1–36.

——: On Classifying Semantic Features. In: *Proceedings of the Tenth International Congress of Linguists*. To be published.

Bolinger, Dwight L.: The Atomization of Meaning. In: *Language* 41, 1965, pp. 555–573.

——: *Aspects of Language*. New York: Harcourt, Brace and World, 1968.

Carroll, John B. (Ed.): *Language, Thought and Reality: Selected Writings of Benjamin Lee Whorf*. Cambridge: M.I.T. Press, 1956.

Chomsky, Noam: *Syntactic Structures*. The Hague: Mouton and Company, 1957.

——: *Aspects of the Theory of Syntax*. Cambridge: M.I.T. Press, 1965.

——: *Cartesian Linguistics*. New York: Harper and Row, 1966.

——: Remarks on Nominalizations. In: Jacobs and Rosenbaum (Eds.):

Readings in English Transformational Grammar. Waltham, Mass.: Ginn-Blaisdell, forthcoming.

Diamond, Jared M.: Zoological Classification System of a Primitive People. In: *Science* 151, 1966, pp. 1102-1104.

Dinneen, Francis P. (Ed.): *Monograph Series on Languages and Linguistics* No. 19. Washington: Georgetown University Press, 1966.

Fillmore, Charles J.: A Proposal Concerning English Prepositions. In: Dinneen (Ed.): *Monograph Series on Languages and Linguistics* No. 19. Washington: Georgetown University Press, 1966.

——: On the Syntax of Preverbs. In: *Glossa* 1, 1967, pp. 91-125.

——: The Case for Case. In: Bach and Harms (Eds.): *Universals in Linguistic Theory*. New York: Holt, Rinehart and Winston, 1968.

Fodor, Jerry A., and Jerrold J. Katz (Eds.): *The Structure of Language: Readings in the Philosophy of Language.* Englewood Cliffs, N. J.: Prentice-Hall, 1964.

Ginsburg, Seymour: *The Mathematical Theory of Context-Free Languages.* New York: McGraw-Hill, 1966.

Gleitman, Lila: Coordinating Conjunctions in English. In: *Language* 41, 1965, pp. 260-293.

Greenberg, Joseph H. (Ed.): *Universals of Language*, Cambridge: M.I.T. Press, 2d ed. 1966.

Jacobs, Roderick, and Peter S. Rosenbaum (Eds.): *Readings in English Transformational Grammar*. Waltham, Mass.: Ginn-Blaisdell, forthcoming.

Jespersen, Otto: *Analytic Syntax*. New York: Holt, Rinehart, and Winston, 1969.

Katz, Jerrold J.: *The Philosophy of Language*. New York: Harper and Row, 1966.

——: Recent Issues in Semantic Theory. In: *Foundations of Language* 3, 1967, pp. 124-194.

——, and Jerry A. Fodor: The Structure of a Semantic Theory. In: *Language* 39, pp. 170-210. Reprinted in Fodor and Katz (Eds.): *The Structure of Language*, Englewood Cliffs, N. J.: Prentice-Hall, 1964, pp. 479-518.

——, and Paul M. Postal: *An Integrated Theory of Linguistic Descriptions.* Cambridge: M.I.T. Press, 1964.

Klima, Edward S.: Negation in English. In: Fodor and Katz (Eds.): *The Structure of Language*, Englewood Cliffs, N. J.: Prentice-Hall, 1964, pp. 246-323.

Lakoff, George: *The Nature of Syntactic Irregularity*. Cambridge: Harvard Computational Laboratory, 1965.

——, and Stanley Peters: Phrasal Conjunction and Symmetric Predicates. In: *Report 17 to the National Science Foundation*. Cambridge: Harvard Computational Laboratory, 1966, pp. VI.1-VI.49.

Langacker, Ronald W.: French Interrogatives: A Transformational Description. In: *Language* 41, 1965, pp. 587-600.

——: *Language and Its Structure: Some Fundamental Linguistic Concepts.* New York: Harcourt, Brace and World, 1968.

——: Pronominalization and the Chain of Command. In: Reibel and Schane (Eds.): *Modern Studies in English*, Englewood Cliffs, N. J.: Prentice-Hall, forthcoming.

Langendoen, D. Terence: The Syntax of the English Expletive "It." In: Dinneen (Ed.): *Monograph Series on Languages and Linguistics* No. 19. Washington: Georgetown University Press, 1966.

——: The Accessibility of Deep (Semantic) Structures. In: Jacobs and Rosenbaum (Eds.): *Readings in English Transformational Grammar*. Waltham, Mass.: Ginn-Blaisdell, forthcoming a.

——: Formal Linguistic Theory and the Theory of Automata. In: Bever and Weksel (Eds.): *The Structure and Psychology of Language*. New York: Holt, Rinehart and Winston, forthcoming b.

Lees, Robert B.: *The Grammar of English Nominalizations* (Publication 12 of the Research Center in Anthropology, Folklore, and Linguistics). Bloomington and The Hague: Indiana University Press and Mouton and Company, 1960.

Lenneberg, Eric: *Biological Foundations of Language*. New York: John Wiley, 1967.

Luce, R. Duncan, Robert R. Bush, and Eugene Galanter (Eds.): *Handbook of Mathematical Psychology*, Vol. II. New York: John Wiley, 1963.

Lyons, John: *Introduction to Theoretical Linguistics*. New York: Cambridge University Press, 1968.

McCawley, James D.: The Role of Semantics in a Grammar. In: Bach and Harms (Eds.): *Universals in Linguistic Theory*. New York: Holt, Rinehart and Winston, 1968.

McNeill, David: 1966. Developmental Psycholinguistics. In: Smith and Miller (Eds.): *The Genesis of Language*. Cambridge: M.I.T. Press, 1966, pp. 15-84.

Miller, George A., and S. Isard. Free Recall of Self-Embedded English Sentences. In: *Information and Control* 7, 1964, pp. 292-303.

Nida, Eugene A.: *Toward a Science of Translating*. Leiden: E. J. Brill, 1964.

Reibel, David A., and Sanford Schane: *Modern Studies in English*. Englewood Cliffs, N. J.: Prentice-Hall, 1968.

Rosenbaum, Peter S.: *The Grammar of English Predicate Complement Constructions*. Cambridge: M.I.T. Press, 1967.

Ross, John R.: *Constraints on Variables in Syntax*. Cambridge: M.I.T. (Ph.D. dissertation), 1967a.

——: On the Cyclic Nature of English Pronominalization. In: *In Honor of Roman Jakobson*. The Hague: Mouton and Company, 1967b.

Russell, Bertrand: *Introduction to Mathematical Philosophy*. London: George Allen and Unwin, 1916.

Sebeok, Thomas A. (Ed.): *Current Trends in Linguistics, Vol. III: Theoretical Foundations*. The Hague: Mouton and Company, 1966.

Slobin, Dan I.: The Acquisition of Russian as a Native Language. In: Smith and Miller (Eds.): *The Genesis of Language*. Cambridge: M.I.T. Press, 1966, pp. 129-148.

Smith, Carlota S.: Determiners and Relative Clauses in a Generative Grammar of English. In: *Language* 40, 1964, pp. 37-52.

Smith, Frank, and George A. Miller (Eds.): *The Genesis of Language.* Cambridge: M.I.T. Press, 1966, pp. 129-148.

Taaffe, James G.: *A Student's Guide to Literary Terms.* Cleveland: World Publishing Company, 1967.

Thorne, J. P.: English Imperative Sentences. In: *Journal of Linguistics* 2, 1966, pp. 69-78.

Watt, William W.: *A Short Guide to English Usage.* Cleveland: World Publishing Company, 1967.

Weinreich, Uriel: Explorations in Semantic Theory. In: Sebeok (Ed.): *Current Trends in Linguistics, Vol. III.* The Hague: Mouton and Company, 1966a, pp. 395-477.

——: On the Semantic Structure of Language. In: Greenberg (Ed.): *Universals of Language.* Cambridge: M.I.T. Press, 1966b, pp. 142-216.

——: On Arguing with Mr. Katz: A Brief Rejoinder. In: *Foundations of Language* 3, 1967, pp. 284-287.

GLOSSARY

Abstract Predicate. A predicate for which a predicate in a clause subordinate to it is substituted by a transformation. Upon substitution, the subordinate predicate may take on a morphological appearance which is different from that of the predicate when it does not undergo substitution. Numerous examples are given in Chapters 6 and 7.

Accessibility. The ease with which the deep structure underlying a particular surface structure of a sentence in a language can be grasped by fluent speakers of that language upon presentation of the sentence.

Adjective. A part of speech of English which occurs as a predicate of an argument of the predicate *be*, and which may not be substituted transformationally for an indefinite pronoun. See Chapter 6 for further discussion.

Agent. An animate noun phrase (in a sentence) whose referent is responsible for the action indicated by the verb.

Ambiguity. Property of a sentence or lexical item having two or more distinct meanings.

Animate. Designating a subcategory of nouns referring to objects having life, but excluding plants. Indicated by the semantic-feature specification [+Animate]. Opposed to INANIMATE, which refers to plants and objects not having life, indicated by the specification [−Animate].

Antecedent. See PRONOUN.

Antonymy. The relation that holds between two lexical items that have the opposite specification for a single binary feature, all other specifications being identical.

Apposition. An expression occurring after a noun phrase and having exactly the same reference as that noun phrase. Traditionally, only a noun phrase may be in apposition to another noun phrase, as in the sentence:

> Mary, my cousin, is here.

In this book, we also consider nonrestrictive relative clauses to be in apposition to noun phrases, as in the sentence:

> Mary, who is my cousin, is here.

See also RELATIVE CLAUSE.

Argument of a predicate. A noun phrase which is a member of the same constituent as that predicate.

Article. A part of speech which, in English, indicates whether the exact reference of the following noun has been established.

Auxiliary verb. Any of those verbs, including the modal auxiliaries, *do*, *have*, and *be*, which precede, rather than follow, the negative constituent, and which occur at the beginning of an interrogative sentence, or immediately following an interrogative word.

Binary feature. See SEMANTIC FEATURE.

Black box. Metaphoric term for anything about which we know only its responses (or outputs) to stimuli (or inputs). We know nothing about its internal structure.

Causative. Designating a two-place predicate which asserts that the state of affairs described in one of its arguments is brought about by the agent named in the other.

Clause. A constituent (of a sentence) which is itself categorized as a sentence. Thus any grammatical linguistic object is a clause; it is referred to as a MAIN CLAUSE to distinguish it from clauses which can make up only a part of it and which serve as arguments to predicates. The latter are referred to as SUBORDINATE CLAUSES.

Collective. See NUMBER.

Conjunct. One of the constituents joined to others of the same category by a conjunction.

Conjunction. A part of speech which serves to connect deep-structure noun phrases and sentences; in surface structure it serves to connect any pair of constituents of the same kind.

Conjunction reduction. The effect of a transformation which operates on conjoined sentences so as to delete repeated occurrences of the same constituents and to rearrange the resulting constituent structure appropriately.

Constituent-membership rule. A rule of grammar which specified what constituents constitute a given grammatical category and in what order. For example the rule:

$$A \to B\ C$$

states that the category A is made up of the constituent B followed by C. Also called a CONSTITUENT-STRUCTURE RULE or PHRASE-STRUCTURE RULE.

A CONSTITUENT-STRUCTURE GRAMMAR is one which is made up entirely of constituent-structure rules, and a CONSTITUENT-STRUCTURE LANGUAGE is one which can be generated by a constituent-structure grammar.

Coreferential. See REFERENT.

Covert semantic-feature specifications. Those which are not associated with particular morphemes of their own, but which are understood to be present along with the other features of particular lexical items. Thus the specification [+Causative] is covertly present in the item *soften* in the sentence:

> The pianist softened his touch.

Cross classifying. Designating semantic features for which all possible combinations of specifications are possible.

Deep level. Representation of the semantic form of a sentence. The structure of a sentence at this level of representation is called DEEP STRUCTURE.

Derivation. The result of substituting a noun, verb, or adjective for abstract predicates other than those involved in inflection. Typically, derivation results in a change in the part of speech, for example the noun *admission* from the verb *admit*. See also INFLECTION.

Diagraming. See PARSING.

Dialect. The variety of a language spoken and comprehended by people of a particular geographical area and/or social class. See also IDIOLECT, STANDARD LANGUAGE.

Direct object. See OBJECT.

E-grammatical; E-ungrammatical. See GRAMMATICALITY.

Elicitation. Technique of obtaining intuitions of grammaticality from fluent speakers of particular languages. Such persons are called INFORMANTS.

Ellipsis. Deletion of deep-structure constituents which are either repetition of constituents elsewhere in the sentence or are otherwise understood from the context.

Extensive approach. Over-all examination of relatively many and diverse sentences of a language.

Extraposition. The copying of a clause at the end of the clause in which it is contained, together with deletion of the original clause or replacement of it by a pronoun—in English, *it*.

Generate. To produce sentences and the grammatical structure associated with them; said of a grammar. The LANGUAGE GENERATED BY A GRAMMAR is set of sentences generated by it.

Genitive case. The form of a noun phrase when it occurs as a constituent of another noun phrase. When it precedes the head noun of the bigger NP, the case is indicated by the suffix spelled *'s* or *'*. When it follows the head noun, the case is indicated by the preposition *of*, and the NP may or may not have the suffix attached; whether or not it does depends on the syntactic origin of the postnominal phrase. The genitive NP may arise from a relative clause introduced by *who/which has*, as in the following examples, in which the genitive noun phrase is italicized:

> *John's* collection is outstanding.
> The collection *of John's* is outstanding.

Or the genitive NP may come directly from a deep structure argument of the head noun, as in the following examples:

> *The general's* widow is still beautiful.
> The widow *of the general* is still beautiful.

The prenominal genitive form of the personal pronouns are suppletive: *my, your, his, her, our, their;* the postnominal forms are: *mine, yours, his, hers, ours, theirs.*

Grammaticality. Property of a linguistic object which is generated by a particular grammar. Such an object is thereby a sentence of the language generated by that grammar. In this book, a sentence of standard present-day American English is said to be E-GRAMMATICAL; a linguistic object which is not a sentence of standard present-day American English is E-UNGRAMMATICAL.

Grammatical transformation. See TRANSFORMATION.

Head of a phrase. The verb of a verb phrase, or the noun of a noun phrase.

Hierarchy of semantic-feature specifications. The fact that given certain feature specifications, for example [+Human], other specifications are unnecessary (or redundant), for example [+Animate, −Abstract].

Idiolect. The variety of a language used by an individual. See DIALECT.

Immediate-constituent analysis. See PARSING.

Imperative. Disignating an English sentence type which is the expression of a command. Such a sentence contains in its deep structure an abstract imperative predicate.

Inanimate. See ANIMATE.

Inapplicability of a transformation. The fact that a transformation cannot be applied to a structure which does not SATISFY the conditions under which it may be applied.

Inappropriate semantic feature. See UNSPECIFIED SEMANTIC FEATURE.

Inchoative. Designating a one-place predicate that asserts that the state of affairs described in its argument comes about.

Indefinite pronoun. See PRONOUN.

Indirect object. See OBJECT.

Infinitive. A subordinate clause whose main verb is not inflected for tense but which must under certain syntactic conditions be preceded by the prefix *to*. The INFINITIVE-CLAUSE SEPARATION TRANSFORMATION has the effect of taking the subject and predicate of an infinitive apart, and under certain conditions putting them at opposite ends of the sentence in which it occurs.

Inflection. Traditionally defined as the forms taken on by nouns and adjectives in declension and by verbs in conjugation. In Chapter 7 we described the inflected forms of a verb in English as those which arise from substitution for the abstract tense or infinitive predicates. The inflected forms of a noun in English are taken to be its singular, plural, and genitive forms.

Informant. See ELICITATION.

Inherent feature. See SEMANTIC FEATURE.

Instrumental. A predicate which, like the causative, asserts that a state of affairs is brought about. It also contains an argument which specifies the instrument by which it is brought about.

Intensive approach. Detailed examination of the syntactic properties of relatively few sentences of a language.

Internal contradiction. The assignment of two incompatible semantic features to a noun phrase within a sentence. Such a sentence is called INTERNALLY CONTRADICTORY. See also SEMANTIC FEATURE.

Interrogative. Designating a sentence type containing the abstract interrogative predicate which has as arguments the speaker (the one who is asking the question) and the content of the question.

Intonation pattern. The pattern of changes in the pitch and intensity of the voice during the utterance of a sentence. This pattern is governed by the surface structure of the sentence.

Intransitive. See TRANSITIVE.

Introspection. Form of elicitation in which the informant is the linguist himself. See ELICITATION.

Language. The set of sentences generated by a grammar. The language spoken and comprehended by humans, sometimes also called NATURAL LANGUAGES to distinguish them from man-made "languages" invented for computer technology, are each made up of an infinite number of sentences. Associated with each sentence is at least one deep structure and a surface structure.

Lexical item. An element of the LEXICON, the units which enter into syntactic combination in sentences. See also WORD.

Linguistic intuitions. Subconscious knowledge which fluent speakers of a language have of that language. When obtained by elicitation, they form the data for the linguist who studies that language.

Linguistic object. Anything which potentially could be a sentence of a language; the linguist's "universe of discourse."

Main clause. See CLAUSE, SENTENCE.

Modality. Designating the possibility, probability, obligation, necessity, or truth value of a proposition. Modality is indicated in English by various one-place predicates, including the MODAL AUXILIARY VERBS: *will, would, shall, should, may, might, can, could, must, ought.* The latter are specially distinguished morphologically by not undergoing inflection in the present tense.

Morpheme. See MORPHOLOGY.

Morphology. The study of the general rules which govern the spoken or written form of sentences of a language. The units of morphological study are known as MORPHEMES. The phonological elements which enter into combination to form morphemes are called PHONEMES. Morphemes quite often, but not invariably, correspond to lexical items, elements which are associated with semantic-feature specifications. Lexical items may, however, comprise groups of morphemes.

Negative. Designating an element which expresses the denial of some proposition; also the sentence type containing that element. In Chapter 6 the suggestion that negation be treated as a predicate is raised, but no decision on the matter is reached there.

Nonrestrictive relative clause. See RELATIVE CLAUSE.

Noun. A part of speech in English which occurs as a predicate of an argument of the predicate *be*, but which may be substituted by a transformation for an indefinite pronoun which carries with it referential capacity. See Chapter 6.

Noun phrase. See PHRASE.

Number. The designation of the size of the referential index of a noun phrase. If the NP has a single referential index, then it is said to be SINGULAR in number; if it has a conjunction of indices, then it is PLURAL in number. A COLLECTIVE noun phrase, for example, *the group*, is singular in number, since reference is being made to a single entity, even though it is made up of a conjunction of individuals.

Object. The noun phrase or phrases which typically follow the verb in clauses. In English, the distinction between DIRECT OBJECTS and INDIRECT OBJECTS is usually made in the following terms. The direct object is directly involved in the action of the verb, while the indirect object specifies to whom or for whom the action of the verb is performed. In the following sentences the direct object is italicized, the indirect object put in small capitals.

> Ace Distributors sells *fishing rods* TO SPORTING-GOODS STORES.
> Ace Distributors sells SPORTING-GOODS STORES *fishing rods*.
> Ace Distributors sells *fishing rods*.
> Ace Distributors sells TO SPORTING-GOODS STORES.

Obligatory transformation. A transformation which must be applied to a structure that satisfies it.

Optional transformation. A transformation which may be, but is not necessarily, applied to a structure that satisfies it.

Overt semantic-feature specifications. Those which are associated with particular morphemes, such as [+Inchoative] in the lexical item *soften*.

Parsing. The analysis of a sentence into its constituents. Also known as IMMEDIATE-CONSTITUENT ANALYSIS or DIAGRAMING. The results of parsing may be displayed, as in Fig. 2.1, in the form of a TREE-DIAGRAM.

Part of speech. One of the traditionally established categories into which words, or lexical items, are classified. These include noun, verb, adjective, adverb, pronoun, preposition, and conjunction.

Passive. A sentence type in which the surface-structure subject has undergone an action or is in a particular state. Such sentences contain the auxiliary verb *be* followed by a past participle.

Perfect aspect. Indication that a state or action held or took place prior to a specified point in time. It is expressed in sentences by the auxiliary verb *have* followed by a past participle.

Person. The reference of an NP with respect to the speaker or writer and the one(s) addressed. If the reference of an NP includes the speaker or writer, the NP is said to be first person. If it includes the one(s) addressed, but not the speaker or writer, it is second person. If it includes neither speaker or writer nor the one(s) addressed, it is third person.

Phoneme. See MORPHOLOGY.

Phrase. A constituent of a sentence intermediate between a clause and the lexical items constituting the clause. The most commonly recognized phrases are NOUN PHRASES and VERB PHRASES. A noun phrase is typically composed of a noun and its modifiers, including relative clauses; a verb phrase is said to be made up of a verb, its modifiers, and its object noun phrase or phrases. See also CLAUSE.

Phrase-structure rule. See CONSTITUENT-MEMBERSHIP RULE.

Plural. See NUMBER.

Predicate. 1. The verb phrase of a sentence (Chapter 3). 2. The deep-structure category which, together with arguments, constitutes sentences. Surface-structure nouns, verbs, and adjectives are all predicates (Chapter 6).

Preposition. A part of speech which expresses the spatial, temporal, or other relationship of the following noun phrase to a predicate elsewhere in the sentence. The preposition together with the noun phrase that follows it is said to make up a PREPOSITIONAL PHRASE.

Progressive aspect. Indication that an action is in progress at a specified point in time. Expressed by the auxiliary verb *be* followed by a present participle.

Projection problem. The problem of determining how the meaning of a constituent can be determined by rule from the meanings of its parts. Semantic projection turns out to be the same process as selection under the view adopted in Chapters 5 and 6 that all semantic-feature specifications are selectional. They could equally well be called PROJECTIVE.

Pronoun. A part of speech that substitutes by means of a PRONOMINALIZATION TRANSFORMATION for an entire noun phrase occurring elsewhere in the sentence or discourse. The latter is called the pronoun's ANTECEDENT. In the conception of deep structure given in Chapter 6, every noun phrase except those composed solely of sentences contains as its head an INDEFINITE PRONOUN which bears the referential index of that noun phrase.

Referent. That to which a noun phrase refers. The indication of the referent is by means of a REFERENTIAL INDEX. Two noun phrases with the same referent are COREFERENTIAL; they have the same referential index.

Relative clause. A clause which is part of a noun phrase and which modifies the head noun of that noun phrase. The deep structure of the relative clause contains an occurrence of the noun it modifies, which appears in its surface structure as a RELATIVE PRONOUN. A RESTRICTIVE RELATIVE CLAUSE restricts or narrows the reference of the noun it modifies; a NONRESTRICTIVE, or APPOSITIVE, RELATIVE CLAUSE does not.

Restrictive relative clause. See RELATIVE CLAUSE.

Rule schema. An abbreviation of an infinite number of rules of grammar as a single rule. Thus the rule schema:

$$S \rightarrow C\ S^*$$

represents the rules:

$$S \rightarrow C\ S\ S$$
$$S \rightarrow C\ S\ S\ S$$
$$\cdots$$

Satisfaction of the conditions of a transformation. See INAPPLICABILITY OF A TRANSFORMATION.

Selectional feature. See SEMANTIC FEATURE.

Self-embedded. Said of a clause which is completely contained within another clause; for example the clause, is self-embedded in sentence (1), but not in sentence (2):

    (1) The notion that massive bodies attract one another is well understood.

    (2) The notion is well understood that massive bodies attract one another.

Semantic feature. A distinguishable element of the meaning of a lexical item, for example Animate. Particular lexical items are SPECIFIED for values of the feature; BINARY semantic features are those whose values can be symbolized by "plus" and "minus." In Chapter 5, a distinction is made between INHERENT feature specifications, for example [+Animate], which are said to subcategorize the lexical item so designated, and SELECTIONAL feature specifications, for example [__[+Animate]], which impose the specification [+Animate] on the constituent following the designated lexical item in a sentence. In Chapters 5 and 6 it is argued that all semantic features are of the selectional type.

Sentence. A basic or "primitive" concept in linguistics:

1. The grammatical category (abbreviated S) which invariably occurs at the starting point of a tree-diagram.
2. A grammatical linguistic object.

See also LANGUAGE, GRAMMAR, GRAMMATICALITY, LINGUISTIC OBJECT, CLAUSE.

Sentence type. A group of sentences all sharing the same property or properties. The property may be the presence of a particular abstract predicate, the number of arguments of the main predicate in the sentence, and so forth.

Singular. See NUMBER.

Specified. See SEMANTIC FEATURE.

Standard language. A dialect of a language which is determined in part by rules of grammar which are explicitly known and taught; it is used within a particular country for broadcasting, publishing, and communication among speakers of different dialects. Typically, standard languages arise from urban, upper-class dialects, and are maintained by spokesmen from the socially elite against drastic change.

Stem. A morpheme to which prefixes and suffixes may (or must) be added to form words.

Strict subcategorizational feature. A syntactic feature of lexical items indicating the syntactic contexts in which they are or are not permitted to occur.

Strong verb. A verb which forms its past and past participial forms with no suffixes but by internal vowel modification.

Subject. The noun phrase which typically precedes the verb in clauses. It can usually be thought of as the constituent which is in focus in a sentence, that which is being talked about or described.

Subordinate clause. See CLAUSE.

Suffix. A lexical item which is not itself a word but only occurs after and attached to a stem, so that it may be at the end of a word.

Suppletive form. An inflected form of a lexical item which bears little or no morphological resemblance to other inflected forms of that item. For example, *went* is a suppletive past tense form of the verb *go*, which historically goes back to the past tense of the verb stem *wend*.

Surface level. Representation of the manifest form of a sentence. The structure of a sentence at this level of representation is called SURFACE STRUCTURE.

Symmetric predicate. A predicate (in sense 2 of the definition of PREDI-CATE) which occurs in deep structure with a plural argument. The predicate asserts a relationship between the referents of that argument which remains the same no matter which one is selected to be subject.

Tense. A one-place predicate indicating the time at which the action or state of its argument took place. It is indicated morphologically in English in a large variety of ways; see Chapter 7.

Transformation. A rule of grammar which has the effect of deleting constituents and/or copying constituents or features of a sentence elsewhere in the sentence. More fully, GRAMMATICAL TRANSFORMA-TION.

Transitive. A subcategory of verbs which occur with object noun phrases. Referred to by the strict subcategorizational feature [__NP]. According to the view presented in Chapter 6, a transitive predicate is any two- or three-place predicate. Opposed to transitive is INTRANSITIVE, a subcategory of verbs which occur without object noun phrases. Referred to by the strict subcategorizational feature [__]. According to the view of Chapter 6, an intransitive predicate is any one-place predicate.

Tree-diagram. See PARSING.

Unmarked feature specification. The specification which a constituent unspecified for a feature takes on when the syntax requires it to have a specification for that feature.

Unspecified semantic feature. A feature which plays no role in the semantic structure of a lexical item and receives no specification in the representation of that item. The feature is furthermore INAPPROPRIATE in case the lexical item is so specified for other features that no specification for that feature can be imposed on it without an internal contradiction arising.

Variable. A member of the grammatical category which ultimately occurs as the head of every noun phrase in deep structure, according to the view expressed in Chapter 6, footnote 2.

Verb. A part of speech in English which occurs as a predicate but never as one which is in an argument of the predicate *be* (see Chapter 6).

Verb phrase. See PHRASE.

Weak verb. A verb which forms its past and past participial forms with the suffix spelled -*(e)d* or -*t*.

Word. A morpheme or group of morphemes which can be readily isolated (and pronounced in isolation) by fluent speakers of a language as a unit of that language. To some extent, this is a matter of convention, since despite the fact that many fluent speakers have no difficulty in isolating and pronouncing the suffix -*ing*, this suffix is not considered a word. In other cases, matters are even more involved. Thus the suffix -*ism* is not generally a word, but in present day standard English it is occasionally treated as such.

PROBLEMS

An asterisk in front of a problem or part of a problem indicates that it is considerably more difficult than those not so marked.

Examples are indicated by letters of the alphabet, and reference to them is made as follows: example 3.e means example e of Problem 3.

chapter 2

1. Describe the internal contradiction in each of the following sentences. Describe the way (or ways) in which the contradiction may be resolved.

   a. The child is the father of the man.
   b. Wisdom takes good care of her sons.
   c. The new car chewed up the miles without difficulty.

2. Find the definition of *zeugma* in a good dictionary, or glossary of literary terms (for example Taaffe [1967]). Redefine the notion in terms of internal contradiction. How are each of the following instances of zeugma interpreted?

   a. That child is as sharp as a tack.
   b. Professor Smith's mind equals the sun in brilliance.
   c. I am happier than a fairy-tale ending.
   d. The old man had a big house and even bigger fits of rage.

3. Paraphrase the various senses of the following ambiguous sentences.

   a. The lamb is too hot to eat.
   b. John discovered what I have in my hand.
   c. What bothered John was being ignored by everyone.
   d. The houses are crowded on the east side of town.

e. The police found the criminals running toward the railroad station.

f. Your argument demonstrates your incompetence.

g. I know more beautiful women than Mary.

h. I know what stories my uncle tells.

i. Bobby wants to replace the Pope.

4. Not all sentences having surface-level structures like that of 2.37 express commands. Other sentences having such structures express advice, possibility, or condition. Classify the following sentences according to what they express.

a. Show respect for your elders, and you will be shown respect when you are old.

b. Go directly to bed and stay there.

c. Win $1000 in the new Bonanza Sweepstakes.

d. Take lots of color film with you when you visit Greece.

e. Show me ten men who are stout-hearted men, and I'll soon show you ten thousand more.

f. Smile and the whole world smiles with you.

g. To get your refund, fill out this form and mail it to the business office downtown.

h. Take this pill as soon as you begin feeling nauseated.

i. Remain in your seats until the plane has come to a complete stop at the terminal.

chapter 3

1. The structure associated with sentences generated by a constituent-structure grammar can be represented in a variety of notations other than that of tree-diagraming. One of these is the labeled bracket notation; the labeled bracketing corresponding to the tree diagram shown in Fig. 3.2 is:

a. $[_S [_{NP} [_N politicians_N]]_{NP} [_{VP} [_V know]_V [_{NP} [_S [_{NP} [_N voters_N]$ $[_{VP} [_V prefer]_V [_{NP} [_N results]_N]_{NP}]_{VP}]_S]_{NP}]_{VP}]_S$

State the structures associated by grammar 3.4 with sentences 3.5 and 3.6 in the labeled bracketing notation. Is any information lost from a labeled bracketing if the labels are left off all the right-hand brackets? Why or why not?

2. In order to study the properties of grammars made up of rules of constituent membership, it is useful to construct "artificial" languages whose lexicon consists simply of the words a, b, c, etc.

Determine the language generated by the following grammars:

a. S → A S B
   S → A B
   A → a
   B → b

b. S → A S A
   S → B S B
   S → A A
   S → B B
   A → a
   B → b

c. S → A S B
S → A C B
C → B C A
C → B A
A → a
B → b

3. Consider the constituent-structure grammar having the following rules:

S   → NP VP
VP → V NP
VP → V PP
PP → P NP
NP → Art N
N   → troops, region
V   → entered, moved, approached, withdrew, circled, landed, skirted, invaded, lived, inhabited, left
P   → in, into, from, around
Art → the

Diagram the structures associated by this grammar with the following sentences.

a. The troops entered the region.
b. The troops moved into the region.
c. The troops left the region.
d. The troops withdrew from the region.
e. The troops inhabited the region.
f. The troops lived in the region.

What is wrong with the structures associated by the grammar with these and other *E*-grammatical sentences which it generates? Would matters be improved any if the grammar treated a verb followed by a preposition as a constituent? Why or why not?

chapter   4

1. Discuss the relationship between the notions selection and projection. Can they be considered two terms for the same notion?

2. Can you think of any other unmarked semantic-feature specifications for English besides [+Male]?

3. What are some examples in English of lexical items whose grammatical and semantic gender or number do not coincide?

4. Provide lists of verbs which select subjects or objects which may be either [1 Penetrable] or [2 Penetrable]; [2 Penetrable] or [3 Penetrable]; which involve a change of state of penetrability of its subject or object.

5. Consider the sentence:

a. The farmer dusted the crop while his wife dusted the floor.

Either the verb *dust* is two lexical items each with a separate meaning, or it is one item with a single meaning, the exact nature of which can only be determined from the context. Which view do you find more satisfying? Why? If you hold to the first view, can you think of a sentence in which *dust* is used ambigiously?

*6. In the text, we asserted that a noun such as *wife* imposed the feature [−Male] on its subject and [+Male] on its object, in order to account for the fact that in the sentence:

    a. That person$_1$ is the wife of the mayor$_2$.

that we understand the referent of *that person* to be female and of *the mayor* to be male. But of course we know more about these referents than just that; in particular, we know that they are married. To account for this, we might wish to associate a relational feature to *that person*, something like [Married to *the mayor$_2$*] and to *the mayor*, something like [Married to *that person$_1$*]. Provide a notation for representing the fact that the subject and object of *wife* are understood to be married to one another. If you succeed in obtaining such a notation, attempt a representation of the semantic content of other kinship terms, such as *husband, spouse, parent, father, son, brother, uncle* (include both the senses "parent's brother" and "husband of parent's sister"), *grandson, nephew.*

Warning: Notice that in the case of the last four terms, the existence of parties other than those named in the sentences in which such terms occur must be assumed. For example, in the case of *brother*, a common parent must be assumed.

*7. Provide a semantic representation of the terms *widower, divorcé, bachelor, fiancé.* For purposes of simplicity, assume that all marriages are monogamous.

chapter 5

1. Extraposition of infinitives is possible under certain circumstances. Consider the following examples and state what you think are the conditions under which such extraposition may take place.

    a. It's possible for anything to disappear around this place.
    b. For anything to disappear around this place is possible.
    c. *Anything is possible to disappear around this place.
    d. It would be desirable for me to lose some weight.
    e. For me to lose some weight would be desirable.
    f. *I would be desirable to lose some weight.

*A more complicated situation is presented by the following examples.

g. It might be wise for you to disappear for a few days.
h. For you to disappear for a few days might be wise.
i. You might be wise to disappear for a few days.

First it must be ascertained whether sentence 1.i has the same meaning (that is, same deep structure) as that of 1.g and 1.h. If not, what is the difference in their deep structures? What transformations do 1.g and 1.h undergo, and what ones does 1.i undergo? What other adjectives besides *wise* enter into constructions like those of 1.g–1.i? Here is a partial list: *nice, thoughtful, nasty*. What other constructions do these adjectives enter into?

2. Consider the kind of extraposition that takes place in sentences such as the following.

a. It's awful the price you have to pay for tomatoes in the winter.
b. It's a disgrace the way he behaves when he's drunk.
c. It's marvelous the amount of weight I've lost since I started on the diet you recommended.
d. It never ceases to amaze me the size dress my neighbor wears.

Describe in what ways the extraposition exhibited in these examples differs from that discussed in the text. This extraposition takes place in the environment of a particularly specified semantic class of adjectives, nouns and verbs. Characterize that class. Hint: consider the ungrammaticality of:

e. *It's high the price you have to pay for tomatoes in the winter.

3. One of the "classic" transformations in English is known as particle movement. Its application can be seen in the following examples.

a. Our friends put us up overnight.
b. The club intends to keep foreigners out.
c. I helped pick the man that the thieves knocked down up.

Compare:

d. *Our friends put up us overnight.
e. The club intends to keep out foreigners.
f. I helped pick up the man that the thieves knocked down.

State the conditions which satisfy this transformation and the conditions under which it is obligatory or optional.

4. (Continuation of Problem 3). Consider the examples:

a. No one lives in that building.
b. *No one lives that building in.
c. The wreckers knocked in that building.
d. The wreckers knocked that building in.

One of the structures underlying example 4.c satisfies the particle movement transformation, but not the one underlying example 4.a. Diagram the structures underlying 4.a and 4.c, and indicate how the former fails to satisfy the particle-movement transformation.

Account also for the ambiguity of example 2.28.

5. State the deep structures underlying the following examples. Of the transformations termed extraposition, infinitival-clause separation, *to be*-deletion, and *it*-deletion, which ones have applied to each of them and in what order?

   a.   The instructor made it clear that we were responsible for the assignments.
   b.   The instructor made certain that no one cheated.

*6. Compare the sentences:

   a.   Lila is ecstatic about Nona's having won the scholarship.
   b.   Nona is ecstatic about having won the scholarship.

In sentence 6.b, the subject of the gerund clause *having won the scholarship* is understood to be *Nona;* since it is identical with the subject of the entire sentence, it is deleted. In sentence 6.a, however, it has not been deleted, because there is no occurrence of the NP *Nona* elsewhere in the sentence. Thus we conclude that the subject of a gerund clause may be deleted in case it occurs elsewhere in the sentence in which the clause occurs.

Now consider the sentences:

   c.   Finding that he$_1$ could not escape, the man$_1$ surrendered.

Notice that 6.c cannot be paraphrased by interchanging the pronoun and antecedent:

   d.   *Finding that the man$_1$ could not escape, he$_1$ surrendered.

Provide an explanation for this in terms of the observations in the preceding paragraph. The following sentences are all like 5.c with regard to the apparent obligatory application of backwards pronominalization.

   e.   Knowing that he$_1$ had just a little time to make a decision only paralyzed the man$_1$ further.
   f.   Wanting people to like him$_1$ was John's$_1$ only desire in life.
   g.   To recognize her$_1$ real feelings wasn't easy for Fran$_1$.
   h.   The opportunity for making his$_1$ fortune passed Frank$_1$ by before he realized it.

Extend your explanation to cover these cases as well.

*7. Consider the following sentences in which backwards pronominalization has taken place:

a. Either he₁ eats his supper or Johnny₁ goes to bed.
b. Not only did she₁ insult me, but Mary₁ also accused me of insulting her!
c. He₁ was well liked by the parishoners, but the priest₁ simply couldn't get along with the bishop.

Why are these examples counterexamples to the claim made in the text about the nature of backwards pronominalization in English? Is there any reasonable way of representing the deep structures of these examples such that they are no longer counterexamples to the claim?

*8. How are the following sentences to be related transformationally:

a. I believe that the strike will be over in a week.
b. The strike, I believe, will be over in a week.

Explore as far as you can the properties of the transformational rules needed to account for the properties of sentences like 8.b.

*9. In Langendoen (1966) it is argued that pairs of sentences such as the following have identical deep structures:

a. The studio is hot.
b. It's hot in the studio.

The deep structure subject is taken to be a locative expression, which is optionally extraposed. If the expression is not extraposed, then the locative prepostion (in these examples, *in*) is deleted. Study the arguments in that article carefully, and then investigate whether a similar analysis can be used to account for the properties of sentences introduced by the word *there*, as in:

c. There is a skeleton in the closet.

Alternatively, such sentences could be transformationally obtained from deep structures in which the NP which follows the form of *be* is taken to be the subject. Evaluate the merits of these two approaches.

*10. For some fluent speakers at least, the following sentence has an interpretation which is not internally contradictory:

a. Tom married his childhood sweetheart and so did Sheila.

For such speakers, the interpretation arises when conjunction reduction applies to the deep structure underlying:

b. Tom married his childhood sweetheart and Sheila married her childhood sweetheart.

What is problematic about this fact? Notice also that for such speakers the following sentence is ambiguous:

c. Tom scratched his ear and so did Sheila.

chapter 6

1. (For those who know baseball.) Provide a paraphrase and a diagram of the deep structure of the sentence:

   a. The tying run is at third base.

2. Provide a plausible set of deep structures for the sentences of Problem 3 in Chapter 3.

3. Account for the ambiguity of sentence 3.i in the problems of Chapter 2.

4. Like questions, exclamations can be thought of as containing an abstract predicate, roughly paraphrasable as *I exclaim that* . . . Discuss systematically the differences between the following questions and exclamations:

   a. What stories my uncle tells!
   b. What stories does my uncle tell?
   c. How many stories my uncle tells!
   d. How many stories does my uncle tell?
   e. What a strain my uncle is under!
   f. What strain is my uncle under?

   and account for the unambiguity of the sentences:

   g. I wonder what stories my uncle tells.
   h. I'm amazed at what stories my uncle tells.

   versus the ambiguity of example 3.h in the problems of Chapter 2, repeated below:

   i. I know what stories my uncle tells.

5. What problems for semantic and syntactic analysis are presented by such expressions as *the lonely crowd?* Why is this expression more problematic than *the angry crowd?*

6. Consider the sentences of Chapter 2, Problem 4. In light of the considerations of this chapter, state the deep-structure forms of commands, advice, and conditionals.

*7. According to Austin (1962), a performative verb is one which, if it occurs in the present tense and with a first person subject, performs the act described by the verb, especially if the expression *hereby* is also used. For example, the following sentences contain performative uses of performative verbs:

   a. I hereby pronounce you man and wife.
   b. I bet you five dollars you can't do that again.
   c. I hereby declare the motion open for discussion.
   d. I vote "aye."

   Which of the abstract predicates that have been considered in this chapter can be considered performatives?

   Compare example 7.c with the following sentence as uttered under appropriate conditions by the chairman of the meeting:

   e. The motion is open for discussion.

Why should 7.e be considered to contain an abstract performative predicate in its deep-structure representation?

Do you think it reasonable to suppose that every statement contains a performative use of a particular abstract performative predicate? If so, what is being "performed"?

*8. Show that the following sentence, and sentences like it, are genuine counterexamples to the claim made in Chapter 5 concerning the nature of backwards pronominalization:

a. That photograph of him$_1$ doesn't do Tom$_1$ justice.

What reformulation is required in the statement regarding the conditions under which backwards pronominalization can take place?

*9. Consider the sentence:

a. [The man who took her$_2$ out last week]$_1$ really loves [the girl who despises him$_1$]$_2$.

Show that the substitution of the antecedent NP for the pronoun with identical reference in this sentence leads to an infinite regress. What consequences does this observation have for the view that pronouns transformationally replace the full NP's which are their antecedents?

What alternative views are possible which avoid this infinite regress? See Bach (1968).

*10. Forwards pronominalization cannot really be said to be obligatory (as was maintained in Chapter 5) for after all one would not want to consider a sentence such as the following to be E-ungrammatical:

a. Although Bill$_1$ was unable to get hold of Tom$_2$ all day, Bill$_1$ didn't give up trying.

Indeed, in order to convey the information contained in the following sentence:

b. Since Bill$_1$ was unable to get hold of Tom$_2$ by telephone, Tom$_2$ paid Bill$_1$ a personal visit.

One would not pronominalize both Tom and $Bill$ in the main clause, since the result, which we give below, is interpreted only to mean that Bill paid Tom a visit.

c. Since Bill$_1$ was unable to get hold of Tom$_2$ by telephone, he paid him a personal visit.

Generalize from these examples to a statement of conditions under which pronominalization is inapplicable.

*11. It was pointed out that sentences such as:

a. The chef heated the soup.

is open to a double interpretation. The soup is understood to have become hotter than it was and furthermore it may or may not be considered hot in an absolute sense. Even so, what should the deep structures of sentences such as the following ones be:

    b. The chef heated the soup to 125°F.

    c. The chef heated the soup to the boiling point.

It would appear that phrases of the type *to 125°F*, and *to the boiling point* are incompatible with both the adjective *hot* and its comparative *hotter*. Notice, however, that we can say:

    d. The chef caused the soup to become heated to 125°F.

    e. The chef caused the soup to become heated to the boiling point.

This suggests that rather than having adjectives, such as *hot*, or even their comparative forms, in the most deeply embedded sentence in the deep structure underlying examples such as 11. a, we have, rather, past participles, such as *heated*.

Now, observe that this analysis immediately provides a more intuitively satisfying solution to the problem of such examples as:

    f. The ice cube melted.

Rather than postulate a hypothetical adjective *melt*,† for the most deeply embedded sentence in the deep structure of example 11.f, we may assume that the past participle *melted* occurs there (see footnote 4 of Chapter 6).

The conclusion, however, can be taken to be a *reductio ad absurdum* for the position that inchoative and causative sentences are formed in the manner described in the text, and support for the position adopted in Chomsky (1968) that the deep structures of these sentence types are not complex; that their inchoative or causative character is a consequence of the lexical representation of their main verbs. Discuss.

chapter 7

  1. Describe the phonological relationships between the following verbs and their corresponding nominalizations.

Verb	*Nominalization*
prove	proof
grieve	grief
live	life
relieve	relief
believe	belief
breathe	breath
use	use
advise	advice

  2. Despite morphological appearances, why are the following nouns not related to the corresponding verbs by nominalization?

Noun	*Verb*
strife	strive
mouth	mouthe
ignorance	ignore

3. Occasionally, people coin new verbs out of more complex nominal forms. This process is known as back-formation. A typical instance is the military use of the verb *destruct* (back-formed from *destruction*, itself a nominalization of *destroy*) and its corresponding nominalization *destruct*. Occasionally children and even adults will make use of back-formations with sometimes striking results; for example:

    a. I deducted (= deduced) the answer.
    b. The earth revolutes (= revolves) on its axis.

Record instances of novel back-formations you have heard or have used yourselves.

4. Compare the internal modifications of the English strong-verb conjugation with those of German. Compare the patterns of cognate verbs in the two languages.

5. Account for the ambiguity of the sentence:

    a. Everyone was waiting for Bill's surprise.

Warning: There are at least four interpretations of this sentence.

6. Account for the ambiguity of example 3.f of Problem 3 of Chapter 2.

*7. Investigate the properties of the verbs *dare* and *need* in standard English. State the relationship between their use with marked and unmarked infinitives and their behavior as auxiliary verbs.

INDEX

Many of the terms that appear in the glossary are also indexed below. For such items, the page on which the term appears in the text in small capitals is indicated by italics.